COURSE NOTES

Cour

CW00556188

CONSTITUTIONAL AND ADMINISTRATIVE LAW

John McGarry

Public Law.

Routledge
Taylor & Francis Group

LONDON AND NEW YORK

First published 2014
by Routledge
2 Park Square, Milton Park, Abingdon, Oxon OX14 4RN

and by Routledge
711 Third Avenue, New York, NY 10017

Routledge is an imprint of the Taylor & Francis Group, an informa business

© 2014 John McGarry

British Library Cataloguing in Publication Data
A catalogue record for this book is available from the British Library

Library of Congress Cataloging in Publication Data
A catalog record has been requested for this book

ISBN: 978-1-4441-6691-0 (pbk)
ISBN: 978-0-203-78410-5 (ebk)

Typeset in Goudy and Frutiger
by Wearset Ltd, Boldon, Tyne and Wear
Printed by Bell & Bain Ltd, Glasgow

MIX
Paper from
responsible sources
FSC
www.fsc.org   **FSC® C007785**

Dedication

For Clare, Joe, Joan and Ken with love.

Contents

Guide to the book

Check new words and essential legal terms and what they mean

Definition

Capacity: understanding, awareness, capability, clear mind, reasoning, ability.

Test your legal knowledge! Practice makes perfect – answer questions on what you've just read

Workpoint

Why is capacity important in criminal law?

Questions to help you delve deeper into the law and to guide your further reading

Research Point

In 2003 the Parliamentary Joint Committee on Human Rights criticised the age of criminal liability in their Tenth report of Session 2002–03, HL/1High Court. Look up paragraphs 35–38 and make notes on the main arguments below.

Provides examples and extracts from the key cases and judgements you need to know

Case:	
***Antoine* (2000)**	The words 'did the act or made the omission' in the 1964 act refer to the *actus reus* only. The Mental element need not be explored.

Diagrams illustrate key points for visual learners

People who lack capacity in criminal law

Children under the age of ten

Corporations

Those with a mental illness

Tick off what you have learnt and check you're on track

Checkpoint – corporate manslaughter

Item on checklist:	Done!
I can explain the effect of *C v DPP* (1995) on the doctrine of doli incapax.	
I can suggest ways in which a Crown Court trial could be made more accessible to a child.	

Provide you with potential real-life exam questions.
Answers are available on the accompanying website.

Potential exam questions:

1) Assess the ways in which incapacitated defendants are dealt with in the criminal court system.

2) Examine the role of vicarious liability in criminal law.

3) Corporations can be indicted for criminal offences the same as individuals can. Discuss.

Guide to the website

There is useful additional material online to support your learning of law. http://cw.tandf.co.uk/law/Constitutional-and-Administrative-Law

Interactive questions to help you revise aspects of the law

Model Answers

Chapter 1

1. When the criminal law prosecutes and sentences criminals, its purpose is to:

   • incapacitate the criminal

   • punish the criminal

   • deter the criminal and the public

   • reform the criminal

   • educate the criminal and the public

   • affirm moral standards and restore justice in society

Useful websites to help you research further your studies in law

www.parliament.uk
The official Parliament website; use it to track all criminal bills currently before Parliament, explore the role of the House of Lords in law-making, and search for delegated legislation.

www.legislation.gov.uk
The official website for the Stationary Office; use it to search for newly enacted and revised legislation, draft legislation and statutory instruments for the United Kingdom, Scotland, Northern Ireland and Wales.

Acknowledgements

I would like to thank Jasmin Naim, Lucy Winder and their Hodder colleagues, as well as Damian Mitchell and Emma Nugent at Routledge, for their collective patience, encouragement and advice throughout all stages of this book and for ensuring that the transfer from Hodder to Routledge was, for me at least, trouble-free.

I am grateful to the following for their support, friendship and various child-entertainment duties: Sharyn and Bobby Duffey; Joan and Ken McGarry; Phillipa and Jack Malone; and Gemma Shiels and Phil McNabb. I thank my colleagues Adam Pendlebury and Robert Collinson for their practical help, advice and encouragement. I also thank Gavin Muir, Alex Muir and Alison Haughton for providing me with welcome distractions of badminton and insobriety. Finally, I would like to thank my wife, Clare Kinsella, and son, Joe, for their love, patience, support and, well, everything.

Preface

Constitutional and administrative law is one of the most interesting subjects that students may be asked to study. The rules and principles you will read about in this book shape the way in which we in the United Kingdom are governed and the conduct of those that govern us. Aspects of constitutional and administrative law often form the context and background for many news stories and an understanding of the subject will help you to better understand the news and the world in which we live. Moreover, many of the topics covered in this book are concerned with some of the fundamental protections that the constitution offers us, the citizen, against potential abuse by those in power.

Yet, despite its importance and potential appeal, constitutional and administrative law is a subject with which many students struggle. Such students often see the subject as something to be endured, rather than enjoyed, and they fail to do as well in it as they might.

This book is intended for students of all abilities studying constitutional and administrative law. It will demystify the subject for those who find it difficult and help them better negotiate their way through the various topics, as well as enabling deeper insight for the more confident student. The book contains many aids to help you develop your understanding, including: diagrams; Checkpoints to help you test yourself; clear explanations of key cases; suggestions for further research; and examples of the types of questions on which you may be examined, with suggested answers provided on the companion website. I hope all readers will find this book to be useful in helping them develop their knowledge and appreciation of this area of law.

Table of cases

Table of statutes and other legislation

Statutes

Statutory Instruments

European Legislation

International Legislation

Treaties and Conventions

China

France

United States of America

Chapter 1
Initial matters

In this chapter we will look at some of the concepts that arise when studying constitutional and administrative law. An initial knowledge of these concepts may help you to understand the subject as a whole. The chapter will look at the following:

- the distinction between public law and private law;

- what is usually meant by the terms 'constitutional law', 'administrative law' and 'human rights';

- the component parts of the United Kingdom;

- the European Union and the European Convention on Human Rights.

1.1 Public law/private law

Constitutional and administrative law is also known as public law, and thinking of it in this way, and contrasting it with private law, is a good way to begin to understand the subject.

In essence, private law governs the relationship between private individuals or bodies. So, if you enter into a contract, or if you sue someone for negligence or defamation, you are operating in the realm of private law. If I sell my house or make a will, this is also a private law matter. Similarly, the relationship between my employer and me is a private law relationship.

Public law deals with the different institutions of state (i.e. of government) and the relationship between the state and private individuals and bodies.

We can represent the difference between public law and private law in the following way:

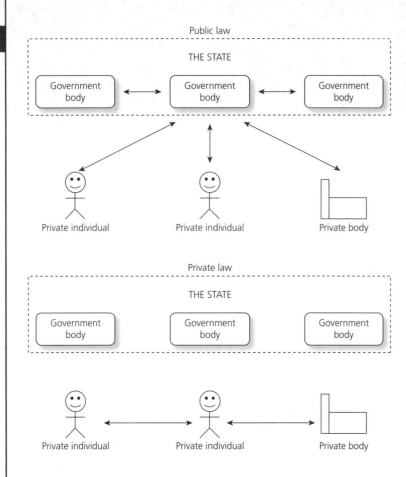

In the above diagrams, the arrows signify the legal relationship between different bodies. In the first, the relationships indicated are public law relationships because the arrows run between different government bodies (which collectively compose the state) and between the state and private individuals or bodies. In the second, the arrows run only between private bodies or individuals indicating private law relationships.

> <u>Note</u>: Public law, as defined above, includes criminal law. However, criminal law is treated as a separate legal area and is taught as such on most if not all courses.

1.2 Constitutional law, administrative law and human rights

The subject to which this book relates is known as 'Constitutional and Administrative Law' or 'Public Law'. Whatever the name given to the subject at the institution at which you are studying, it may be broken down into three parts: constitutional law, administrative law and human rights. It is not always easy to draw a clear distinction among these three areas of law because they tend to blend into each other. Indeed, some would suggest that there is little to be gained from drawing any distinctions and it is unlikely that your lecturer will spend much (if any) time defining or distinguishing them. However, it may be useful for you to have the basic definitions of these areas of law.

- *Constitutional law* is concerned with the relationship between the different institutions of the state and with the source, scope and distribution of the powers of those institutions.

- *Administrative law* is concerned with the control of governmental power. One of the primary ways in which such control is exercised in the United Kingdom is by judicial review (which we will examine in Chapters 10 and 11) whereby the courts ensure that the discretionary power possessed by government bodies, lower courts and tribunals is exercised lawfully.

- *Human rights law* is concerned with the protection of citizens' rights against state intrusion. These rights are often guaranteed by a constitutional document, legislation or a treaty. In the United Kingdom, this protection is primarily provided by two documents: the European Convention for the Protection of Human Rights and Fundamental Freedoms (commonly referred to as the European Convention on Human Rights) and the Human Rights Act 1998. We will look at the protection offered by these two documents in Chapter 12.

1.3 The United Kingdom

You may find it useful to be able to distinguish the various parts that make up the United Kingdom. It is common for people to refer to the United Kingdom and Great Britain interchangeably but these are not synonymous terms. It is also common for (English) students to say or write 'England' when they mean 'United Kingdom'.

A good way to understand the difference between the component parts of the United Kingdom is to think of its full, formal title, which is:

The United Kingdom of Great Britain and Northern Ireland

We can see from this that, while Northern Ireland is part of the United Kingdom, it is not part of Great Britain. To say this in a slightly different way, the United Kingdom is made up of England, Scotland, Wales *and* Northern Ireland, whereas Great Britain is made up of just the first three of these countries: England, Scotland and Wales.

We may represent the composition of the United Kingdom in the following way:

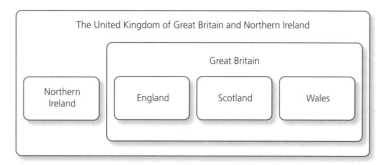

1.4 The European Union and the European Convention on Human Rights

We will look in more detail at the European Union in Chapter 9 and at the European Convention on Human Rights in Chapters 12 and 13. I will therefore give only a brief account here.

1.4.1 The European Union

The European Union is currently made up of 27 member states (i.e. 27 countries). It has had various names and incarnations throughout its history: the Common Market, the European Economic Community (EEC), the European Community (EC) and now the European Union (EU). Indeed, the earlier names of the EU give a good indication of one of its main and original purposes: to create a common market or common economic area. That is, a primary purpose of the EU is to create a single market where there can be a free movement between the member states of people, goods, services and capital. The achievement of this has required the (continuing) harmonisation of the laws of the member states; it has also required the member states to give priority to EU law over their own law.

It would be a mistake, though, to imagine that the EU is simply concerned with facilitating trade; it is, and always has been, more than this. It is not simply an economic union but also a political and social one. To these ends it is developing, among other things, common policies on justice, home affairs and foreign affairs.

We will look at the main institutions of the EU in Chapter 9; however, it will be useful to make a brief note of them here:

- *The Court of Justice of the European Union* is the body tasked with resolving legal disputes within the EU.

- *The European Commission* is concerned with the protection and development of EU law.

- *The European Council* is made up of the heads of government of each of the member states as well as the President of the European Council and the President of the European Commission. Its role is to plan the overall direction of the EU.

- *The Council of the European Union* comprises ministers from each of the member states and its role is to develop policy and legislation.

- *The European Parliament* is made up of MEPs directly elected by the citizens of the member states.

1.4.2 The European Convention on Human Rights

The European Convention on Human Rights (full title: the European Convention for the Protection of Human Rights and Fundamental Freedoms) is a treaty between different countries. There are currently 47 signatories to the Convention; that is, 47 countries have agreed to be bound by the terms of the treaty. These are known as the High Contracting Parties or Signatory States.

Definition

A **Treaty** is an agreement between two or more states (countries) which is governed by international law and to which the states concerned have agreed to be bound.

The signatories to the Convention have agreed to protect certain rights of their citizens and others within their jurisdiction. Some of the rights protected by the Convention are:

- the right to life (Article 2 of the Convention);

- the prohibition of torture and degrading and inhuman treatment (Article 3);

- the right to a fair trial (Article 6);

- the right to respect for one's private life, family life, home and correspondence (Article 8);

- the right of freedom of expression (Article 10).

In addition to the original Convention, there are a number of protocols to which the Contracting Parties may agree and which expand or add to the rights guaranteed by the Convention or alter the way in which the Convention operates. So, for instance, Protocol 13 came into force in 2003 and prohibits, in all circumstances, the imposition of the death penalty.

For our purposes, the two main institutions concerned with the Convention are:

- *The European Court of Human Rights*

  This is a court whose main purpose is to hear and adjudicate on complaints that one of the signatory states has infringed the rights protected by the Convention.

- *The Council of Europe*

  This is an organisation made up of 47 countries whose main purpose is the promotion of democracy, human rights and the rule of law. The primary way in which it achieves these aims is via the European Convention on Human Rights and its associated protocols.

Note!
The Council of Europe (which is primarily concerned with the European Convention on Human Rights) should not be confused with the European Council or the Council of the European Union (which are both EU bodies).

It will be seen from the above that the European Union and the European Convention on Human Rights (or, more correctly, the Council of Europe) are separate legal entities with their own, discrete, legal

Workpoint

Identify as many differences as you can between the European Union and the European Convention on Human Rights.

systems, institutions and membership. It is common for students – and indeed politicians and those in the media – to confuse or conflate the European Union and the European Convention on Human Rights. When students do this in an assessment – in coursework or an exam or other test – they may as well tell the person marking their work that they have only the slightest understanding of things. It is therefore of the utmost importance that you do not make this mistake and that you know the difference between these two legal entities (though I doubt that anyone who has been wise and discerning enough to purchase this book is likely to commit this error).

Checkpoint – initial matters

Item on checklist:	Done!
I can give a brief definition of the distinction between public law and private law.	
I can distinguish constitutional law, administrative law and human rights.	
I can distinguish between England, Great Britain and the United Kingdom.	
I can explain the difference between the European Union and the European Convention on Human Rights.	

Chapter 2
The UK constitution

In this chapter we will examine the following:

- different definitions of the word 'constitution';
- what is meant when we say a constitution is written or unwritten;
- the argument that a constitution should be a superior form of law that is entrenched;
- the argument that a constitution should establish, and so exist prior to, the system of government it regulates;
- ways of characterising constitutions;
- the function of constitutions;
- the question of whether the UK has a constitution.

2.1 Definitions

It will be useful to begin by looking at a number of ways of defining constitutions. One thing to bear in mind here is that there is no universally agreed definition of what a constitution is. We will begin by looking at a simple definition before moving on to some more demanding ones.

A simple definition of a constitution might read:

A constitution consists of the rules and principles that govern an organisation.

The difficulty with such a definition, some might say, is that it is so broad it does not really define anything; the definition is such that it would mean that all organisations, no matter how loose or informal, would have a constitution.

In 2001, the House of Lords Select Committee on the Constitution produced the following, more particular, definition of a constitution:

'Our working definition of a constitution is that it is the set of laws, rules and practices that create the basic institutions of the state and its component and related parts, and stipulate the powers of those institutions and the relationship between the different institutions and between those institutions and the individual.'

(House of Lords Select Committee on the Constitution First Report: Reviewing the Constitution – Terms of Reference and Methods of Working (HL 11, 2001))

We can see that this differs in a number of ways from the first possible definition given above.

- First, it is clear that the word 'constitution' is being used to refer specifically to the laws, rules and practices that govern the basic institutions of the state – the institutions of government – rather than any organisation.

- Second, by this definition, a constitution stipulates the powers that these institutions have and the relationship among them and between the institutions of the state and the citizen.

We should be clear that it is possible, and proper, to talk of other organisations (i.e. not states) having constitutions. So we may say that a local sports club has a constitution. However, in the context of constitutional and administrative law, when we talk of constitutions we will usually be referring to the constitution of a state.

Some commentators would argue that the definition of a constitution given by the House of Lords Select Committee is not sufficient. In a well-known academic article, F.F. Ridley argued that Britain does not have a constitution because it lacks certain 'essential characteristics' of a constitution. These 'essential characteristics' include:

a) a constitutional law that is superior to ordinary law;

b) constitutional rules and principles that are entrenched;

c) a constitution that exists prior to, and so established, the UK system of government.

(F.F. Ridley, 'There Is no British Constitution: A Dangerous Case of the Emperor's New Clothes' (1988) 41 Parl Aff 340)

Most UK commentators would disagree with Ridley's conclusion that Britain (or the UK) does not have a constitution. Yet his argument allows us to consider some questions concerning constitutional characteristics.

- What does it mean to say that constitutional law should be superior to ordinary law?

- What does it mean to say that a constitution should be entrenched?

- What does it mean to say that a constitution should exist prior to, and so establish, the system of government?

We will examine these questions as we progress through the chapter.

2.2 Written and unwritten constitutions

There is another reason why it is sometimes argued that the UK does not have a constitution – namely that the UK does not possess a written constitution.

> **Definition**
>
> **Written constitution:** A country is said to have a written constitution when the fundamental rules by which the country is governed may be found in a single document or a series of related documents.
> **Unwritten constitution:** A country has an unwritten constitution when there is no single document or series of related documents in which the fundamental rules of the government may be found.

Countries that have a written constitution may use the word 'constitution' in two senses: a broad or narrow sense.

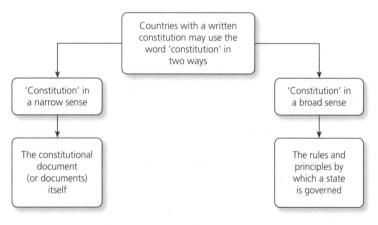

Written constitutions often come into being following some event that has caused a break with the past way of doing things. This might be a revolution, a war or the gaining of independence from, say, a former colonial ruler – peacefully or otherwise.

When such momentous events occur in countries, causing a substantial break with the past, there is often a corresponding need to redraft the rules regulating the government and legal system of that country which then lead to the drafting of a written constitution.

There have been several significant events in the UK's history, including:

• the creation of the UK itself with the Treaty of Union between the Kingdoms of England (which included Wales) and Scotland in 1707 to create the United Kingdom of Great Britain and then the Act of Union 1801 to include the Kingdom of Ireland to form the United Kingdom of Great Britain and Ireland;

• the secession of southern Ireland from the United Kingdom in the first half of the twentieth century, creating the Irish Free State (later Republic of Ireland) and leaving the United Kingdom of Great Britain and Northern Ireland;

• the abdication of the throne by Edward VII in 1936 and his replacement by his brother George VI (the father of the present Queen, Elizabeth II);

• the extension of the voting franchise so that all adult men and women are entitled to vote (with some exceptions such as prisoners or those lacking mental capacity) and other extensions of political rights – particularly to women;

• devolution of law-making and governmental power to Scotland, Wales and Northern Ireland;

• the enactment of the Human Rights Act 1998.

Yet such changes have largely been developments of what exists rather than new beginnings. The one possible exception to this is the establishment under Oliver Cromwell of the Commonwealth of England in 1649 (and of England, Scotland and Ireland in 1653), which followed the English Civil War and the execution of Charles I. Even this, though, did not in the end represent a substantial, long-lasting break with the past. It was, rather, more of a relatively short interlude. This is because the Commonwealth was abolished and the monarchy restored after the death of Cromwell and a brief rule by his son.

In short, the history of the UK, unlike that of many countries, has not been such that there has been a perceived need to create a constitution, from the beginning, establishing the whole system of government. Because of this, the fundamental rules by which the country is governed have, at best, developed in an ad hoc, piecemeal fashion. Indeed, it is sometimes said that the UK constitution has not been made but has grown.

The UK is one of only three countries that does not possess a written constitution, the other two being Israel and New Zealand.

Workpoint

List the benefits of the UK adopting a written constitution.

No written constitution can ever provide the answer to all constitutional issues that may arise. The Constitution of the United States of America, for instance, is silent on the questions of whether women have a constitutional right of abortion or whether the prohibition of same-sex marriages is unconstitutional, and yet these are issues with which the US courts have had to grapple on constitutional grounds.

2.2.1 The Cabinet Manual

In 2011, the Government produced the Cabinet Manual. The aim of this document is to be a guide as to the operation of government. Its significance here is that, for the first time, a substantial number (though not all) of the laws and principles of the constitution are contained in one document. That is, the Cabinet Manual details some of the fundamental laws of the constitution in one document in a way that it is claimed a written constitution does (in fact, the Cabinet Manual contains more detail than many written constitutions).

Some may argue that the creation of the Cabinet Manual represents the first step towards a written constitution. The counter-argument to this is that the Cabinet Manual does not have the characteristics usually associated with written constitutions, including:

- It has simply been drafted by the Government to describe, rather than prescribe, what happens.

- It can be altered without much, if any, discussion.

- It is not comprehensive – it describes only the operation of Government.

• It has no legal status.

We will look at the Cabinet Manual again in Chapter 3.

2.3 A superior, entrenched constitution

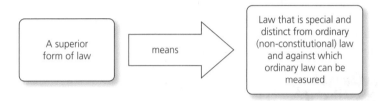

In some countries, constitutional law is seen as a superior form of law. This means that it is recognised as being special and distinct from ordinary law (that is, non-constitutional law). It may also mean that it is the law against which ordinary law may be evaluated and if necessary ruled to be invalid.

In many countries, the courts have the power to strike down legislation that conflicts with the constitution – effectively rendering it null and void. For example, this power is possessed by the German Federal Constitutional Court (the *Bundesverfassungsgericht*) and the Supreme Court of the United States of America.

In those countries where the constitution is a superior form of law, it will also, almost inevitably, be entrenched.

Definition

> **Entrenched:** Entrenched law cannot be altered in the same way as ordinary law; amendment will usually require a special, more onerous procedure to be followed and this will often be prescribed by the constitution itself.

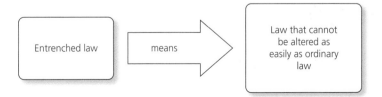

For example, Article 5 of the Constitution of the United States of America establishes the way in which amendments may be made to the constitution and these differ from the way in which non-constitutional change may be achieved.

An entrenched constitution may protect the principles enshrined in the constitution from being easily altered or abandoned to achieve the short-term aims of transient politicians. On the other hand, a constitution that curtails the powers of government may prevent it from taking action that is necessary in the national interest. Moreover, an entrenched constitution may protect principles that were wholly appropriate at the time of drafting but that are anachronistic – out of place – decades or even centuries later.

Workpoint

List the advantages of entrenched constitutions and unentrenched constitutions.

In the UK, it has traditionally been the position that there is no superior, entrenched constitutional law.

Indeed, the famous constitutional theorist A.V. Dicey stated in the nineteenth century that there was an *'absence of any legal distinction between constitutional and other laws'*, meaning that there is no superiority of constitutional over ordinary law and that constitutional law may be altered or repealed in the same way as ordinary law – there are no special procedures for effecting constitutional change (A.V. Dicey, *Introduction to the Study of the Law of the Constitution*, 10th edn, 1959, London: Macmillan [1898]).

This would mean that the Constitutional Reform Act 2005 can be altered in precisely the same manner as the Road Traffic Act 1988 despite the greater constitutional significance of the 2005 Act.

Because constitutional law can be amended in the same way, and just as easily, as ordinary law, the UK constitution is said to be flexible.

Definition

Flexible constitution: Constitutional change is easy to achieve.
Rigid constitution: The procedures for altering the constitution are such that change is difficult to achieve.

One reason why it has historically been thought that the UK does not have any superior, entrenched constitutional law is because of the doctrine of parliamentary sovereignty (we will examine parliamentary sovereignty in Chapter 6).

> **Definition**
>
> **Parliamentary sovereignty:** Traditionally, this is taken to mean that Parliament can enact any law whatsoever and that no court or other body is able to strike down Acts of Parliament or otherwise rule on their validity.

It is questionable whether it is still true to say that the UK does not have a superior constitutional law. Not least because the *obiter dicta* of Laws LJ in the *Thoburn* case, the decision of the Appellate Committee of the House of Lords in the *Factortame* case and various statements from judges suggest that the position has changed.

> **Definition**
>
> *Obiter dicta*: 'Said by the way' – i.e. comments made in the course of giving a judgment.
> *Ratio decidendi*: The reason for a decision.

> Note: Only the *ratio decidendi* of a case is binding precedent (i.e. binding on future cases). *Obiter dicta* are, at best, persuasive authority.

Case:	
***Thoburn v Sunderland City Council* [2003] QB 151**	Facts: This concerned a challenge to legislation that made it an offence to sell loose goods – such as fruit and vegetables – in imperial, rather than metric, measurements. Held: The challenge to the legislation failed. The judge, Laws LJ, stated that there is a *'hierarchy of Acts of Parliament'* and made a distinction between *'ordinary'* statutes and *'constitutional'* statutes. Moreover, he said that the implied repeal rule will not apply to constitutional statutes in the same way that it applies to ordinary statutes.

Definition

> **The implied repeal rule:** Where two Acts of Parliament conflict, the one that has been enacted later will be taken to repeal (to revoke) the earlier one to the degree necessary to resolve the conflict.

In the *Thoburn* case, Laws LJ gave some examples of constitutional statutes, including the European Communities Act 1972 (the legislation that incorporated EU law into UK law) and the Human Rights Act 1998 (which made some of the rights protected under the European Convention on Human Rights part of, and available in, UK law).

If Laws LJ is correct (bearing in mind that his comments are *obiter* only), the traditional view that there is no superior constitutional law in the UK is no longer accurate.

In addition, if he is also correct to claim that the implied repeal rule does not apply to 'constitutional' statutes, then such statutes cannot be amended or repealed as easily as 'ordinary' statutes, which means that constitutional statutes are – to a small degree at least – entrenched.

Example

Imagine that in 2011 Parliament enacts the (fictional) Courts Act, section 1 of which states: '*In making a determination on any matter, courts shall not take into account any judgment or decision of any body or court not based in the United Kingdom.*' This (fictional) provision would conflict with section 2 of the (real) Human Rights Act 1998, which reads:

A court or tribunal determining a question which has arisen in connection with a Convention right [i.e. those rights protected under the European Convention of Human Rights via the Human Rights Act] must take into account any ... judgment, decision, declaration or advisory opinion of the European Court of Human Rights.

That is, section 2 of the Human Rights Act instructs the UK courts to take into account judgments, decisions etc. of a court not based in the UK: the European Court of Human Rights.

- The implied repeal rule would normally dictate that, because the (fictional) 2011 statute was enacted at a later date than the 1998 Human Rights Act, it would impliedly repeal the earlier legislation to the degree necessary to resolve any conflict between them.

- Yet, if Laws LJ is correct, because the Human Rights Act 1998 is a constitutional statute, the implied repeal rule does not apply, and it will remain unaltered by the (fictional) 2011 Act.

- According to Laws LJ, express words are needed to amend a constitutional statute so that, if section 1 of the (fictional) 2011 Act simply stated: 'Section 2 of the Human Rights Act 1998 is hereby repealed' – that is, if it used express words to repeal the provision in the 1998 Act – then this would successfully repeal the section.

While Laws LJ's comments in the *Thoburn* case may be *obiter* only, they seem commensurate with the decision of the House of Lords in the earlier *Factortame* case.

Case:	
R v Secretary of State for Transport, ex parte Factortame Ltd and Others (No. 2) [1991] AC 603	The courts prevented part of the Merchant Shipping Act 1988 from taking effect because it conflicted with EU law.

The importance of the *Factortame* decision is that it seems to conflict with the doctrine of parliamentary sovereignty, noted earlier, which prevents the courts from overriding Acts of Parliament. It also suggests that the courts will give preference to EU law over a conflicting Act of Parliament.

We will revisit the *Thoburn* and *Factortame* cases in Chapter 6 when we look at parliamentary sovereignty in more detail. For now it is sufficient to note that both cases suggest that it may no longer be entirely correct to claim that the UK has no superior, entrenched constitutional law.

We should not overstate this. Any entrenchment is very modest and would not prevent a simple majority in Parliament achieving constitutional change if it wished to do so. In fact, recent years have seen substantial constitutional change including:

- devolution of some law-making and governmental power to Scotland, Wales and Northern Ireland;

- the creation of a UK Supreme Court to replace the Appellate Committee of the House of Lords as the final court of appeal in the UK;

• the removal of all but 92 hereditary peers from the House of Lords (prior to this, over 700 hereditary peers had the right to sit and vote in the Lords).

These changes would be viewed as hugely significant in any country and yet they have been achieved in the UK by ordinary Acts of Parliament.

2.4 A constitution that establishes the government

I noted above that Ridley argues that a constitution should establish, and so exist prior to, the system of government.

Ridley's argument echoes that of the eighteenth-century writer and revolutionary Thomas Paine who stated that 'A *constitution is a thing antecedent to a government*' and that a '*government without a constitution is a power without right*'.

For example, in 1787, representatives of 12 of the 13 states that at that time composed the United States of America met and devised a new constitution. The result of their deliberations is still the basis of the whole of the political, governmental and legal system of the United States.

Yet, as we have already noted, in the UK there has not been an event that has given rise to the desire to establish or re-establish the fundamental rules by which the country should be governed. Rather, the system of government has simply developed and altered to meet changing circumstances. As a result, it could be said that the UK constitution simply describes what is rather than what should be; that is, it describes rather than prescribes.

Workpoint

List the possible reasons why some might consider it desirable that a constitution is prior to and so establishes the system of government.

The argument that a constitution should be prior to the government it establishes is, in part, an argument of legitimacy. That is, some would suggest that a government without a pre-existing constitution is not legitimate or, as Paine might say, is exercising power without right.

Also, where a constitution exists before, and establishes, the system of government, it will dictate the manner in which it should operate and is likely to impose limits on its power. So, like the argument that a constitution should be entrenched and superior to ordinary law, the contention that it should be prior to the government is one based on limiting governmental power. The concern is that, without such pre-existing limits, governments may be over-mighty and abuse their powers.

2.5 Constitutional characteristics

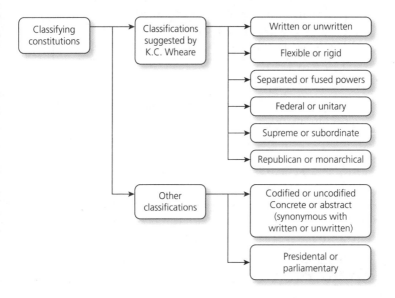

We have seen that constitutions may possess different characteristics. They may, for instance, be written or unwritten, flexible or rigid, etc. It will be useful to look again at these and other ways by which we may describe or classify constitutions. A good starting point is to use the six classifications suggested by the academic K.C. Wheare.

• *Written or unwritten*

We have already noted that a written constitution is one in which the main rules of the constitution are contained in one document or series of related documents; an unwritten constitution is one where there is no such document or documents.

• *Flexible or rigid*

This relates to the ease with which the constitution may be altered.

> Note: A constitution that is flexible in theory may prove
> to be rigid on some matters in reality. For instance, the
> UK's constitution is considered to be very flexible but it
> may be difficult to make some particular changes
> because of a lack of political or popular will. Consider, as
> an example, a proposal to abolish the monarchy. In
> theory, this could be achieved by a simple Act of
> Parliament but the reality is that such a change is unlikely
> because it would lack the necessary support. Likewise, a
> constitution may be rigid in theory but particular changes
> may be easy to achieve in practice because there is
> sufficient agreement that the amendment is desirable.

• *Separated or fused powers*

It is common for the governmental powers of a country to be
divided into three – executive power, legislative power and judicial
power – and for these powers to be exercised by three different
bodies: the executive (the Government), the legislature (Parliament) and the judiciary (Courts). There is a separation of powers
when these different functions are exercised by different bodies.
There is a fusion where some or all of these functions are exercised
by the same body or where the members of one body (say, the executive) are also members of another body (say, the legislature).

Workpoint

Why do you think it is considered desirable that the powers of
government are separated and exercised by different bodies?

We will look in more detail at the concept of separation of powers in
Chapter 5.

• *Federal or unitary*

A federal constitution is one where the power of the state is divided
between central (sometimes known as federal) government and local
(or state) government and where this division of power is fixed by the
constitution so that it cannot be altered without an amendment to the
constitution. An example of a federal state is the United States where
the powers of government are divided between the federal and state
governments and each are prohibited by the constitution from
encroaching upon, or exercising, the power of the other. A unitary
state is one where state power is ultimately possessed by central

government. There may be local bodies that exercise governmental powers but these powers will be granted, and may be removed, by central government. Thus, in a unitary state, the division of power between central and local government is not fixed by the constitution.

• *Supreme or subordinate*

A constitution is supreme when it is not subject to, or limited by, any external authority. A constitution is subordinate when it is subject to some superior external power that may amend it.

• *Republican or monarchical*

A monarchical constitution exists where the head of state is a monarch. This is the case even if the role of the monarch is largely ceremonial, i.e. even if the monarch exercises little or no political power. A republican constitution is one where the head of state is a president. Like a monarch, a president's powers in a republic may be largely ceremonial; this is the case, for example, with the President of the Republic of Ireland.

Wheare's six classifications are a useful way to think about and describe constitutions. It is worth noting three other possible ways to classify constitutions.

• *Codified or uncodified*

Some writers have suggested this classification as an alternative to the written/unwritten dichotomy. Their rationale is that a constitution may be uncodified, in the sense that the fundamental rules are not contained in a constitutional document or series of documents, but that large parts of it may be written in, say, legislation or case reports. By the same token, a constitution may be described as codified because the fundamental constitutional principles are contained in one document but much of it may, in fact, be unwritten.

• *Concrete or abstract*

Like the previous classification, some writers suggest the classification 'concrete or abstract' rather than 'written or unwritten'. A concrete constitution is one where the main rules are contained in a constitutional document (or documents) and an abstract constitution exists where this is not the case.

• *Presidential or parliamentary*

A presidential system is one where the head of government is not part of the legislature (parliament). The United States is an example of such a system: the President is not part of the legislature (Congress) and, indeed, is prohibited from being so by the constitution. A parliamentary system is one where the head of government is a prime minister who is a member of the legislature and is accountable to it for the government's actions.

It is worth noting here that the French constitution is unusual in that it is a mix of both presidential and parliamentary systems. The President is not part of the legislature but chooses, as a member of his government, a Prime Minister who is.

> <u>Note</u>: Strictly speaking, the Queen is the head of government in the UK (it is Her Majesty's Government) but she exercises very little personal political power and the reality is that, for all intents and purposes, the Prime Minister is the head of government.

Workpoint

Classify the UK constitution according to the following classifications:

Written or unwritten
Codified or uncodified
Concrete or abstract
Flexible or rigid
Separated or fused powers
Federal or unitary
Supreme or subordinate
Republican or monarchical
Presidential or parliamentary

2.6 The functions of a constitution

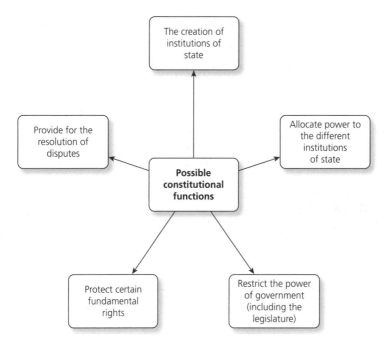

One way to think about constitutions is to ask what role we want a constitution to perform. That is, what do we want the constitution to do?

There are a number of different functions that we may think a constitution should perform (some of these are implicit in the discussion in this chapter so far), including:

- A constitution should facilitate the creation of different institutions of state.

- A constitution should allocate power among the various institutions of state, deciding which bodies should exercise which powers.

- A constitution should restrict the power of the government (including the legislature) and should therefore prohibit certain laws and actions. This argument for limited government is sometimes referred to as 'constitutionalism'.

Definition

Constitutionalism: The view that governmental power derives from and should be limited by the constitution.

- A constitution should provide for the resolution of disputes that arise between citizens (including private bodies or organisations), between citizens and government and between different elements of government.

- A constitution should protect certain fundamental rights of its citizens.

Of course, many of these functions are interrelated. For example, a constitution that protects certain rights of its citizens against intrusion by the state will also be one that limits the state's power (by preventing it from intruding upon those rights).

Workpoint

How, if at all, are the following functions undertaken in the UK?

Note: It might be the case that the function in question is not undertaken in the UK.

Function:	How it is achieved
The creation of different institutions of state	
The allocation of power to the different institutions of state	
The limitation of governmental power	
The resolution of legal disputes between: citizens; citizens and the state; different elements of the state	
The protection of human rights	

2.7 Does the UK have a constitution?

The question of whether the UK has a constitution is an old one; it is also one to which your lecturer is likely to make some reference and which may even make the subject of one of your assessments, either in coursework or an examination.

I should also note that most UK academics and lawyers (including me) are likely to be of the view that the UK does have a constitution. This does not mean that you should agree with them. Indeed, as a marker of student work, it is refreshing when I read a student's work that differs from my own views on a matter, as long as the work is well-argued and substantiated. Whatever your answer, this is a useful question to ask because it allows consideration to be given to the nature and characteristics of the UK constitution.

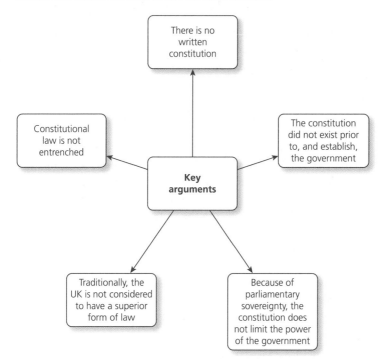

A good starting point is to consider why the question of whether the UK has a constitution might arise at all. We have met some of these arguments above but it will do no harm to remind ourselves of them here and to look at some possible counter-arguments.

• **Most countries have a written constitution; the UK does not.**

Possible counter-arguments

One could try to challenge this by arguing that much of the UK's constitution is, in fact, written because many of its rules and principles can be found in Acts of Parliament, case law and (recently) the Cabinet Manual.

However, I think that there is a more effective challenge to this criticism and that is to question whether the absence of a written constitution (as traditionally conceived) is as significant as may be claimed. To do this, we might imagine that an Act of Parliament is enacted that contains all the existing major rules of the UK's system of government and states that these rules are to be known as the 'Constitution of the United Kingdom'. Presumably, those who had previously argued that the absence of such a document meant that there is no constitution would then concede that one exists. Yet, given that nothing of substance would have changed, one may ask whether the presence of a written document is as necessary as is sometimes asserted.

- **It is argued that a constitution should establish, and so exist prior to, the government; this is not the case in the UK where the system of government has developed organically.**

Possible counter-arguments

Again, one can challenge whether this does mean that the UK does not have a constitution. One can do this by making a comparison with a country where it is not in doubt that a constitution exists but where it can also be said that there have been changes to that constitution. For instance, we may point out that the Constitution of the United States of America has been amended 27 times (and these amendments did not exist before the system of government) yet this piecemeal development is not said to invalidate it in the way that the ongoing development of the UK constitution is said to do. In short, the point is that all constitutions adapt to meet changing circumstances and so it should not be a criticism of the UK constitution that it also does this.

- **It is argued that the constitution should limit the power of government but the UK principle of parliamentary sovereignty means that there are no legal restrictions on the laws that may be enacted.**

- **It is often claimed that constitutional law should be a superior form of law; historically, this has not been the case in the UK.**

- **It is suggested by some that the constitution should be entrenched but in the UK constitutional law can be amended as easily as non-constitutional law.**

Possible counter-arguments

These three points are very similar and may be taken together. We may first point out that, as noted above (Section 2.3), it may no longer be accurate to claim that in the UK there is no superior, entrenched constitutional law or that Parliament may alter any law just as easily as another.

Second, and perhaps more convincingly, we may suggest that these are arguments for a particular *type* of constitution, i.e. one that is superior, entrenched and limits the power of the state. We may then ask why it should be thought that a constitution should have these particular characteristics and not others. That is, we can contend that this is a matter of political choice, and that the citizens (or their representatives) of a country should be free to choose to organise their affairs in a different way. They may, for example, choose to adopt an all-powerful legislature that can enact any laws whatsoever, including laws that alter the constitution, as we have in the UK. In short, one could suggest that arguments for a particular type of constitution should not be confused with arguments about whether there is a constitution.

In the end, like many of the questions you will meet in this subject, there is no right or wrong answer to the question of whether the UK does or does not have a constitution. As a student, perhaps the best that you can do is understand why the question arises, be able to discuss various characteristics of constitutions in general and the UK's constitution in particular, and make an interesting and well-argued answer to the question if asked.

Checkpoint – Constitutions

Item on checklist:	Done!
I can give a definition of a constitution.	
I know what is meant when people claim that constitutional law should be a superior or higher form of law.	
I know what is meant when people claim that a constitution should be entrenched.	
I know what is meant when people claim that a constitution should establish, and so exist prior to, the system of government.	

Checkpoint – Constitutions

Item on checklist:	Done!
I can understand the following classifications: • written and unwritten • codified and uncodified • concrete and abstract • flexible and rigid • separated and fused powers • federal and unitary • supreme and subordinate • republican and monarchical • presidential and parliamentary.	
I can give at least four functions that it is claimed a constitution should perform.	
I can give an account of why some people argue that the UK does not have a constitution.	

Potential exam question

The UK not only has a constitution, it has a written constitution. Discuss.

Chapter 3
Constitutional conventions

We will look at the following in this chapter:

- what constitutional conventions are and their significance in the UK constitution;

- some prominent examples of constitutional conventions;

- definitions of constitutional conventions;

- the development, usefulness and characteristics of constitutional conventions;

- the courts and constitutional conventions;

- possible codification of constitutional conventions.

3.1 The importance of constitutional conventions

It just so happens that many of the most important rules of the UK constitution are not legal rules at all but are constitutional conventions. Let's look at an example.

In May 2010, there was a General Election in the UK.

> **Definition**
>
> **General Election:** An election where all the seats in the House of Commons are contested.

The result of this election was that no party had an overall majority of seats in the House of Commons; that is, no party had more than 50 per cent of the Members of Parliament (MPs). After a few days of negotiation among the three main political parties – the Conservatives, Labour and the Liberal Democrats – the Conservatives and

Liberal Democrats agreed to form a coalition government under David Cameron (leader of the Conservatives) as Prime Minister.

The question arises: what is the rule governing who becomes Prime Minister of the United Kingdom?

The rule is not, as people sometimes think, that the person who wins the general election becomes Prime Minister.

• In the first place, in the UK, we vote for MPs to represent us in the House of Commons rather than directly electing prime ministers.

• Second, it may be the case that we have a change of prime minister even though there has not been a General Election.

For example, in 1990 John Major became Prime Minister (succeeding Margaret Thatcher) and in 2007 Gordon Brown became Prime Minister (succeeding Tony Blair), yet there was no general election in 1990 or 2007.

The rule is that the Queen will appoint as Prime Minister the person who can command a majority of support in the House of Commons.

It will be appreciated that this is a fairly important rule of the UK constitution – because it determines who leads and forms the government – but (and this is the point) it is not a legal rule at all. It is a constitutional convention.

Indeed, if the Prime Minister could no longer command a majority of support in the House of Commons, but refused to resign, one could not begin legal action to remove him or her. This is because the rule governing who is Prime Minister is not a legal rule and the courts will only enforce legal rules.

Given the above, we may adopt an initial definition of constitutional conventions:

Constitutional conventions are non-legal rules that govern the operation of various aspects of the constitution.

This initial definition will suffice for now but we will revisit it below and look at how others have defined conventions.

All constitutions will be governed, to some degree, by constitutional conventions that modify the way in which the legal aspects of the constitution work in practice. In the UK they are particularly significant because they determine the way things actually operate to a greater extent than in most countries. It is therefore important that one has an understanding of them to appreciate how things really work because an understanding of only the legal position would be misleading.

Legal rules of the constitution	may be modified by	Constitutional conventions Non-legal rules of the constitution

For example, legally speaking the UK has a very powerful monarch who is able to exercise a great deal of political power directly and personally. In fact, the Queen is under no legal obligation to appoint a Prime Minister to head her Government. Yet the legal position is modified by constitutional convention so that the Queen's personal political powers are, in reality, tightly circumscribed and her legal powers are largely exercised on her behalf by the Prime Minister and other ministers.

> Note: The word 'convention' is being used in a particular way here. It should not be confused with the meaning of the word in everyday usage, to mean a customary way of acting or a gathering of a group of people. Also, *you must never* mistake the European Convention on Human Rights for a constitutional convention; this is a common mistake made by students and it indicates a lack of understanding. The European Convention on Human Rights is an agreement between states to protect the rights of those within their control; it is *not* a constitutional convention.

3.2 Some examples of constitutional conventions

It may be useful to examine some prominent examples of constitutional conventions to get a feel for their importance in the UK constitution and for how they operate.

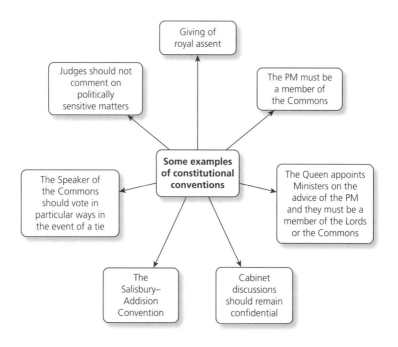

- *Royal assent*

    Generally speaking, an Act of Parliament must be passed by the House of Commons, the House of Lords and receive royal assent from the monarch (there are some exceptions to this under the Parliament Acts 1911 and 1949 whereby an Act may be passed without the agreement of the House of Lords (see Section 6.3.1)).

    The legal position, then, is that the Queen is free to grant or withhold her Assent as she chooses. However, the legal position is modified by a constitutional convention that states that the monarch must give Assent to an Act of Parliament when advised to do so by her ministers.

> Note: The last monarch to personally grant Assent to legislation was Queen Victoria in 1854. Nowadays, Assent is granted on the monarch's behalf by Lords Commissioners or (more commonly) by a written order, known as a letter patent.

- *The Prime Minister must be a member of the House of Commons*

I noted above that there is no legal requirement for the Queen to appoint a Prime Minister at all. However, by convention one is appointed. Moreover, convention dictates that the Prime Minister must be a member of the House of Commons.

At one time, the Prime Minister could be chosen from either the House of Lords or the House of Commons. The last Prime Minister to be appointed from, and remain in, the House of Lords was Lord Salisbury, who held the office from 1895 until 1902. In 1963 Lord Home (pronounced 'Hume'), a member of the House of Lords, became Prime Minister. By this time it was thought unacceptable that the Prime Minister should not be a member of the Commons and so Home renounced his peerage and was successfully elected to the House of Commons. It is now unthinkable that the Prime Minister would not be a member of the Commons.

This example tells us something interesting about constitutional conventions: generally, they form and crystallise over time (there are some exceptions to this; see the Salisbury–Addison convention below). At some point between 1902, when Lord Salisbury left office, and 1963, when Alec Douglas-Home became Prime Minister, a constitutional convention emerged requiring the Prime Minister to be a member of the House of Commons rather than the Lords.

- *All ministers must be a member of the House of Commons or the House of Lords and are appointed by the Queen on the advice of the Prime Minister*

Legally, the Queen may appoint whomever she likes as a minister, whether they are a member of either House of Parliament or not. This legal position is modified by the conventional rules that require that the Queen acts on the advice of the Prime Minister when making ministerial appointments and that all ministers must be a member of either the House of Commons or the House of Lords. If the Prime Minister wants to appoint someone as a minister who is not a member of one of the Houses of Parliament, then that person must seek election to the Commons or be appointed as a peer in the House of Lords.

For example, in 2008, the then Prime Minister wanted Peter Mandelson to rejoin the Labour Government. At the time, Mr Mandelson was not a Member of Parliament, so, in order to facilitate his appointment as a minister and conform to the conventional rule, he was made a peer (i.e. a member of the House of Lords), becoming Baron Mandelson, of Foy in the County of Herefordshire and Hartlepool in the County of Durham – more commonly referred to as Lord Mandelson.

• *Discussions in Cabinet should remain confidential*

We will consider this convention again in the next chapter but its essence is that discussions between ministers should remain confidential so as to best facilitate an open exchange of views. However, this convention is often breached and ministers will 'leak' the views expressed by their colleagues to the press.

Definition

The Cabinet: The decision-making body at the head of the executive. It is made up of senior members of the government. In the UK, the Cabinet comprises the Prime Minister and other senior ministers.

• *The Salisbury–Addison convention*

This states that the House of Lords will not block Government legislation which is being enacted to fulfil a manifesto commitment (i.e. a promise made by a political party as part of its election campaign). This convention was the result of a statement by Viscount Cranborne (the 5th Marquess of Salisbury from 1947) in 1945. The reason it was thought necessary was because in the general election of 1945 the Labour Party had won a majority of the seats in the House of Commons and so formed the government. Yet, the House of Lords at that time was made up almost entirely of hereditary peers and the overwhelming majority of these belonged to the Conservative Party which could use this majority to prevent the government enacting legislation. That is, it was considered illegitimate in the modern age that the unelected part of the legislature could block legislation passed by the elected part.

Definition

The hereditary principle: Where membership of the body in question (e.g. the House of Lords) passes from one family member to the next.

The Salisbury–Addison convention is particularly interesting because it demonstrates two particular things about constitutional conventions:

a) Conventions generally develop to adapt to changing circumstances while leaving the legal position unchanged. In this case it was felt to be no longer appropriate, given that the UK was becoming a more democratic country, that unelected peers could block legislation enacted by elected representatives and on which the electorate can be said to have voted.

b) While most conventions develop over time and it is not always possible to identify when they solidified into a rule, the Salisbury–Addison convention shows that this is not always the case and that they may be created by a positive act that can be pinpointed at a particular time.

- The Speaker of the House of Commons does not vote unless it is necessary to break a tied vote, in which event the Speaker's actions are themselves governed by convention

Legally, the Speaker is free to vote however he or she wishes but, again, this legal position is governed in practice by the constitutional convention that states that the Speaker should not vote unless this is necessary to break a tie. When there is a tie the Speaker should use his or her casting vote according to three principles:

a) He or she should vote in the way that best facilitates further discussion.

b) Where further discussion is not possible, he or she should not vote for a decision unless this is supported by a majority.

c) A casting vote on an amendment to proposed legislation should leave that legislation in its original form, i.e. it should be a vote against the amendment.

> **Definition**
>
> **The Speaker of the House of Commons:** An MP who is the Presiding Officer of the House and whose role includes chairing proceedings and ruling on matters of propriety and procedure. The Speaker is elected by his or her fellow MPs and, once elected, is expected to act impartially and to sever affiliation with their former party. In General Elections, the Speaker stands for election as Speaker rather than as a member of a political party.

• Judges should refrain from publicly commenting on certain matters

Generally speaking, there is a constitutional convention that judges should publically refrain from commentating on certain matters, including:
• the merits of Government policy;
• the likely effects of proposed legislation;
• the merits of particular holders of judicial, political or other public office.

3.2.1 A US example

It is worthwhile considering an example of a constitutional convention that used to operate in the United States. It was a convention in the United States that no President would serve more than two terms in office; i.e. they would not stand for election again after being elected twice. This practice was started by the first US President and followed by every subsequent President up to Franklin D. Roosevelt in the 1930s and 1940s who stood and was elected as President four times.

The convention was later made into law by the 22nd Amendment to the US Constitution.

This example indicates two things:

a) Constitutional conventions are not simply a feature of the UK constitution; they also govern the operation of other, if not all, constitutions.

b) A breach of a constitutional convention that is considered important may lead to the rule being enacted as a law.

3.3 Characteristics of conventions

The above examples should help you gain an initial understanding of the nature and characteristics of constitutional conventions. From them, we can identify a number of characteristics.

- Constitutional conventions are binding on those to whom they apply.

- Constitutional conventions govern the way that all branches of the state operate: the legislature (Parliament), the executive (Government) and the judiciary (Courts).

- Constitutional conventions are not legal rules and are not enforced by the courts.

- Constitutional conventions are binding in a political sense.

- Constitutional conventions usually develop over time. There are some exceptions to this: for instance, the Salisbury–Addison convention (Section 3.2) began at a particular, and identifiable, point in time.

- Constitutional conventions allow the constitution to adapt to changing circumstances and social mores.

- Constitutional conventions often begin as a political practice that crystallises into a rule and it is not always possible to pinpoint when this has occurred. See, for example, the rule that the Prime Minister must be a member of the House of Commons (Section 3.2).

- Conventions govern the conduct of those who hold public office.

- Constitutional conventions are usually shaped by precedent; that is, past actions govern the present-day conduct of officials.

- Constitutional conventions regulate the operation of most, if not all, constitutions – they govern the way the strict legal position works in practice.

- The consequences of a breach of a constitutional convention depend on circumstances. In some cases, if the convention is considered sufficiently important, the rule may be enacted as a law.

For example, we have already seen a US example of a constitutional convention being enacted as a legal rule in Section 3.2.1, above. We can also look at a famous UK example. There is a constitutional convention that states that if there is a disagreement between the House of Lords and the House of Commons, the Lords should eventually give way to the Commons in recognition of its democratic credentials. This convention is not always strictly adhered to and there are occasional situations where the House of Lords refuses to give way to the House of Commons. This famously happened in 1909 when the House of Lords, in which there was a massive Conservative majority, refused to pass the Liberal Government's Budget which included new proposals for taxing wealthy landowners. The Parliament Act 1911 was enacted as a direct result of this clash between the Commons and the Lords. To some extent, this puts the conventional rule on a statutory footing because it allows legislation to be enacted without the agreement of the House of Lords. We will look at the Parliament Act 1911 (and the Parliament Act 1949) again in Section 6.3.1.

3.4 Definitions of conventions

In Section 3.1, above, I gave an initial definition of constitutional conventions:

Constitutional conventions are non-legal rules that govern the operation of various aspects of the constitution.

It will be instructive here to look at other definitions that have been given. This is because there is not one definition of conventions and there are sometimes significant differences between different definitions. I will look at two well-known definitions that have such differences: one from Dicey and one from Marshall and Moodie.

Dicey:

'The rules which make up constitutional law ... include two sets of principles or maxims of a totally distinct character. The one set of rules are in the strictest sense "laws", since they are rules which ... are enforced by the courts; these rules constitute "constitutional law" in the proper sense of that term, and may for the sake of distinction be called collectively "the law of the constitution".

The other set of rules consist of conventions, understandings, habits or practices which, though they may regulate the conduct of ... officials, are not in reality laws at all since they are not enforced by the courts. This portion of constitutional law may, for the sake of distinction, be termed the "conventions of the constitution"...

... "conventions of the constitution" consists of maxims or practices which, though they regulate the ordinary conduct of the Crown, of ministers, and of other persons under the constitution, are not in strictness laws at all.'

(Dicey, A.V., *Introduction to the Study of the Law of the Constitution* 10th edn, 1959, London: Macmillan [1898])

We can take a number of different things from Dicey's definition.

- Dicey seems to be saying that the constitution is made up of two parts: constitutional law and constitutional conventions. To say this in a slightly different way, for Dicey constitutional law and constitutional conventions seem to make up the totality of the constitution.

Dicey's view:

This position was echoed by the Supreme Court of Canada:

'constitutional conventions plus constitutional law equal the total constitution of the country.'

> (*Reference re Amendment of the Constitution of Canada* (1982)
> 125 DLR (3d) 1)

- Dicey makes it clear that conventions regulate the conduct of those who have a constitutional role, including ministers, the Crown and other officials.

- Conventions are not legal rules and are not enforced by the courts.

- Dicey appears to believe that constitutional conventions are made up of understandings, habits and practices.

We can contrast Dicey's definition with one provided by Geoffrey Marshall and Graeme Moodie:

'By conventions of the Constitution ... we mean certain rules of constitutional behaviour which are considered to be binding by and upon those who operate the constitution but which are not enforced by the law courts (although the courts may recognise their existence), nor by the presiding officers in the Houses of Parliament.'

> (Marshall, G. and Moodie, G., *Some Problems of the Constitution*,
> 5th edn, 1971, London: Hutchinson)

Workpoint

Identify the similarities and differences between Marshall and Moodie's definition of constitutional conventions and Dicey's.

Dicey and Marshall and Moodie are in agreement that constitutional conventions are not enforced by the courts and that they regulate the conduct of those who operate and work in the constitution.

However, Dicey and Marshall and Moodie appear to differ in that the latter state that conventions are binding rules whereas Dicey writes that conventions include '*understandings, habits or practices*'.

What is the difference between understandings, habits or practices and a binding rule? In essence, the obligation imposed by a binding rule is much stronger than that imposed by an understanding, habit or practice. In fact, one might say that there is little, if any, obligation to act in a particular way imposed by either a habit or a practice.

For example, it might be my habit to have a cup of tea at breakfast but no one would argue that, because this is what I usually do, I am under an obligation to always do that; I could not be subjected to legitimate criticism if I decided to have coffee instead of tea one morning.

Workpoint

From your reading so far, which definition do you think best fits with what you take a constitutional convention to be? Can you think of a better definition of your own?

You may find it illustrative to look at the way different writers define constitutional conventions and what the differences and similarities are among the definitions they give.

I believe that most commentators would state that conventions are more than an understanding, habit or practice; most, I suggest, would argue that they impose a strong degree of obligation on those to whom they apply and should therefore be characterised as binding.

3.5 Identifying conventions

If constitutional conventions are to be differentiated from mere practices or habits, then the question arises as to how we may make this distinction.

Workpoint

It is the practice of UK Prime Ministers to live at 10 Downing Street but few would claim that it is a constitutional convention. Why do you think this is?

Sir Ivor Jennings suggested that a constitutional convention could be identified in the following way:

The Jennings test:

'We have to ask ourselves three questions: first, what are the precedents; secondly, did the actors in the precedents believe that they were bound by a rule; and thirdly, is there a reason for the rule?'
(Jennings, I., *The Law and the Constitution*, 1963, London: University of London Press)

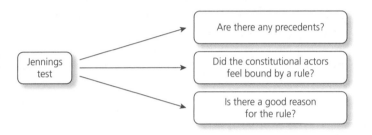

It is worthwhile unpacking the Jennings test a little. First, his test has three aspects:

a) Are there any precedents for the rule? That is, have the constitutional actors acted in the way suggested by the convention in the past?
 • For example, the convention that the Queen will give royal assent to a statute when advised to do so by her ministers is supported by a string of precedents going back centuries.

b) Did the actors in the precedents believe that they were bound by a rule? That is, did the constitutional actors feel under an obligation to act one way rather than another?
 • For example, it is clear that those involved feel that there is a binding rule that the Prime Minister should be a member of the House of Commons rather than the House of Lords.

c) Is there a good reason for the rule? I suggest that Jennings means here: is there a good *constitutional* reason for the rule?
 • For example, there are good constitutional reasons for why, in a modern democracy, a hereditary monarch should not have a personal power of veto over the creation of law.

We should bear in mind that the three aspects of Jennings' test should not be treated as always necessary in the sense that if one element is not satisfied then there is definitely no constitutional convention. Indeed, he made this clear himself:

'A single precedent with a good reason may be enough to establish the rule. A whole string of precedents without such a reason will be of no avail, unless it is perfectly certain that the persons concerned regarded them as bound by it.'

(Jennings, I., *The Law and the Constitution*, 1963, London: University of London Press)

For example, the Salisbury–Addison convention, mentioned in Section 3.2, above, was considered binding from the start even though no precedents for it would have existed at that time.

Alex Carroll has also provided us with a useful way of distinguishing between conventions and things that may simply be considered political practices:

'The fact that a particular political practice has been repeated over a period of time or in a given set of circumstances does not, of itself, elevate it to the status of convention. Thus the traditional ritualistic activities of the Chancellor of the Exchequer on Budget day are too trivial and lacking in constitutional significance to merit the title of convention. Other "usual" practices such as the expectation that the Prime Minister will include in the Cabinet persons from the various wings (left, right, centre, etc.) of the party in power, although of greater significance, may be regarded as too imprecise and laden with political discretion to be defined as rules.'

(Carroll, A., *Constitutional and Administrative Law*, 4th edn, 2011, Harlow: Pearson)

Thus, according to Carroll, a convention has the following characteristics:

- It has constitutional significance.

- It is sufficiently precise.

- It is not overly laden with political discretion to be defined as a rule.

In addition to the above, I suggest the following simple test:

- If a person acts in a way that contravenes the practice in question, could they legitimately be accused of acting unconstitutionally? If so, then it is likely that a constitutional convention exists.

  - For example (building on Carroll's example above), every year on Budget Day, the Chancellor of the Exchequer stands outside number 11 Downing Street and holds aloft his red ministerial case, containing the Budget, so that he can be photographed by the press. If the Chancellor chose not to do this one year, he might be accused of being a poor sport but he could not *legitimately* be accused of acting unconstitutionally. This practice is simply a piece of political theatre staged for the press rather than a constitutional convention.

- By the same token, if the Queen decided to appoint as Prime Minister someone who was not the person who could command the majority of support in the House of Commons then she could *legitimately* be accused of acting unconstitutionally.

3.6 The courts and constitutional conventions

It is often said that the courts will recognise but not enforce constitutional conventions. It is worth giving this some consideration.

Cases:	
***Liversidge v Anderson* [1942] AC 206**	Facts: In the Second World War, Liversidge was detained on the order of the Home Secretary under the Defence (General) Regulations 1939.
	Held: The detention was lawful. The safeguard of liberty was provided by the constitutional convention that requires that the Home Secretary is accountable to Parliament for his actions.
***Carltona v Commissioners of Works* [1943] 2 All ER 560**	Facts: In the Second World War, the minister was given power by the Defence (General) Regulations 1939 to take possession of property if this was considered necessary in the national interest. An order was made requisitioning Carltona's property. Carltona challenged the order on the basis that it had been signed by an official in the Ministry of Works rather than by the minister.
	Held: The requisition was lawful and the court recognised the constitutional convention that ministers are accountable to Parliament for actions taken by their officials.

43

3.6 THE COURTS AND CONSTITUTIONAL CONVENTIONS

Case:	
Attorney-General v Jonathan Cape Ltd [1976] QB 752	Facts: The Government sought an injuction to prevent publication of the diaries of an ex-minister. Held: The constitutional convention that Cabinet discussions should remain confidential could give rise to a legally enforceable duty of confidentiality. In this particular case, however, the court decided that the confidential nature of the diaries had been erased by the passage of time.

In each of these cases the courts did indeed recognise the pertinent constitutional convention. Yet, we could argue that they did more than this.

In the *Liversidge* and *Carltona* cases, the convention of ministerial accountability to Parliament seems to be used to help legitimise the courts' findings that the actions in question were lawful. That is, the convention appears to be part of the rationale of the decisions.

In the *Jonathan Cape* case, the court said that the convention of confidentiality could give rise to a legally enforceable duty of confidentiality.

It could be argued, then, that in each of these three cases the courts did more than merely *recognise* the application of constitutional convention. Rather, the convention was part of the rationale of the courts' findings.

3.7 Why are constitutional conventions obeyed?

This is a question I am often asked by my students: if constitutional conventions are non-legal rules and cannot be enforced by the courts, why are they obeyed by those to whom they apply?

I think there are a number of probable reasons why conventions are obeyed, including the following (more than one of which may apply in any particular case):

• Those to whom the convention applies believe that it is the appropriate way in which they should behave.

• The convention in question may be obeyed in order to avoid accusations of unconstitutional behaviour.

- The convention may be obeyed because of the possible consequences that may follow if it is breached. For example, if the monarch, guided by her own political beliefs, refused to assent to a Bill that had been passed by the House of Commons and the House of Lords then this might bring the legitimacy of the monarchy into question.

- A constitutional actor may believe that if she ignored a constitutional convention on one occasion, a political opponent may feel similarly freed from their conventionally imposed obligations.

3.8 Codification or conversion to law

There may sometimes be disagreement about whether a particular constitutional convention exists or what is required by convention in a given situation. Because of this, it might be thought appropriate that steps should be taken to make constitutional conventions more certain. This could be achieved by codification: by listing the existing constitutional conventions and clearly stating what each requires of those to whom they apply. It may also be achievable by converting constitutional conventions into legal rules; in fact, this might be thought particularly fitting given the importance of some conventions in the UK. Yet, such developments would bring possible disadvantages.

First, it is worth noting that, if we did convert all, or even some, constitutional conventions into legal rules, it is likely that new conventions would develop to govern how these legal rules should operate in practice.

Second, while codification or conversions into law may make conventions more certain, it may diminish their usefulness by making them less flexible. I have noted throughout this chapter that constitutional conventions enable the constitution to develop to meet changing circumstances.

This is recognised by Jennings:

'The short explanation of the constitutional conventions is that they provide the flesh that clothes the dry bones of the law; they make the legal constitution work; they keep it in touch with the growth of ideas.'

(Jennings, I., *Cabinet Government*, 3rd edn, 1959, Cambridge: Cambridge University Press)

So, increased certainty or clarity may result in a loss of flexibility and vice versa.

In short, codification or conversion to law may introduce unwanted solidity, preventing the constitution adapting when appropriate.

3.8.1 The Cabinet Manual

Before the 2010 General Election, the then Prime Minister, Gordon Brown, asked the Cabinet Secretary, Sir Gus O'Donnell, to produce a Cabinet Manual that would be a record of the rules, conventions and laws governing the way Government in the UK operates. This was published in October 2011.

It may be thought that, because the Cabinet Manual includes details of the constitutional conventions that apply to the executive, it effectively codifies and will crystallise them. This may, in turn, reduce their flexibility. That is, it may be thought that the Cabinet Manual will do more than simply describe the way the executive operates, it will also inevitably prescribe how it should operate.

It remains to be seen whether this will happen, though we should note that Sir Gus has stated that the purpose of the Cabinet Manual *'is to guide but not to direct'* (Gus O'Donnell, *Cabinet Secretary Speech on the Cabinet Manual: Constitution Unit Event*).

Checkpoint – constitutional conventions	
Item on checklist:	**Done!**
I can define constitutional conventions.	
I can give examples of prominent UK constitutional conventions.	
I can list the characteristics of constitutional conventions.	
I know the three parts of the Jennings test for identifying constitutional conventions.	
I can explain why constitutional conventions are useful.	

Item on checklist:	Done!
I can explain the courts' attitude to constitutional conventions.	
I can explain why constitutional conventions are obeyed.	
I can discuss the benefits and disadvantages of codifying constitutional conventions or converting them into law.	

Research Point

Read Chapter 8 of the parliamentary report, *Joint Committee on Conventions: Conventions of the UK Parliament* (2006 HL265/HC1212). What things did the Committee recognise might amount to codification? What arguments are made about the benefits and disadvantages of codification?

Potential exam question

It is inappropriate in the twenty-first century that some of the most significant aspects of the UK constitution are governed by non-legal rules.

Discuss.

Chapter 4
Responsible government and accountability

It is considered important that the Government should be accountable, which means that it should explain its actions, defend them and respond to criticism where necessary. In the UK, ministers are collectively and individually accountable to Parliament and the public.

In this chapter we will look at the following:

- the relationship between the Government and Parliament;
- the structure of Government;
- collective and individual ministerial responsibility;
- the distinction between accountability and responsibility;
- the ways in which Parliament holds the Government to account;

> Note: You will find that an appreciation of current affairs, derived from newspapers or other news media, will be particularly useful in helping you understand and do well in this topic.

4.1 Government and parliament

We saw in Chapter 3 that it is a conventional rule that the Prime Minister is appointed by the Queen. He or she will be an MP and will be the person who can command a majority of support in the House of Commons.

The Queen will also appoint other ministers; legally, she can appoint whomever she wants as a minister but, by constitutional convention, she appoints ministers on the advice of the Prime Minister. This means that, for all intents and purposes, ministers are appointed by the Prime Minister.

We also saw in Chapter 3 that it is a constitutional convention that all ministers must be members of either the House of Commons or the House of Lords.

> Note: This does not mean that all parliamentarians are also members of the Government; most MPs and peers are not members of the Government.

The fact that the Prime Minister will be the person who has the majority of support in the House of Commons means that on most issues the Government will usually be able to rely on the support of a majority of MPs. I use the word 'usually' because there may be some issues over which even the Government's own supporters will not give it their support.

4.2 The structure of government

The Government is headed by the Cabinet. This is the primary decision-making body of the Government and comprises the Prime Minister and other senior ministers. Usually 20–25 ministers make up the Cabinet, although its size will vary and its exact composition is a matter for the Prime Minister.

The Cabinet will normally consist of:

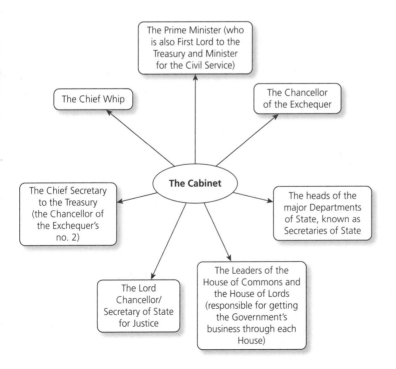

Other ministers may attend Cabinet meetings at the request of the Prime Minister, either regularly or on an ad hoc basis.

In the main, the work of government in the UK takes place through Governmental departments. At the time of writing, the departments that compose the Government are:

These departments will usually be headed by a minister, commonly a Secretary of State, who will have under him or her junior ministers. For instance, at the time of writing, the structure of the Ministry of Justice is as follows:

MINISTRY OF JUSTICE	
Chris Grayling MP Lord Chancellor and Secretary of State for Justice	
Lord McNally Minister of State	Damian Green MP Minister of State
Helen Grant MP Parliamentary Under Secretary of State	Jeremy Wright MP Parliamentary Under Secretary of State

Furthermore, each department will be responsible for a number of specific tasks. So, looking again at the Ministry of Justice, its responsibilities include:

- the administration of the justice system, including funding the work of the courts and the appointment of judges;

- the administration of Legal Aid;

- sentencing policy;

- the administration of prisons;

- probation;

- youth justice.

4.2.1 The Civil Service

The Civil Service is the permanent, non-political part of the Government.

The Civil Service provides the administrative, managerial and technical support that the government needs to pursue its policies.

Civil servants are impartial: they are not political appointees and are expected to serve an administration regardless of its politics. The corollary of this is that civil servants are prohibited from engaging in work that is political in nature.

To illustrate, a civil servant employed as Communications Officer within a department may be expected to inform the press of the work of that department but should not make party political points.

Civil servants are permanent appointments. That is, civil servants will remain in office even if the party in Government changes. So, for example, if the Labour Party forms the next government, there will not be a cull of members of the Civil Service. Members of the Civil Service remain in office when there is a change of government and will serve the new administration as effectively as the previous one.

The *Civil Service Code* sets out the standards that all civil servants are expected to uphold, including standards of integrity, honesty, objectivity and impartiality.

Civil servants are accountable to ministers.

4.2.2 Special advisers

Ministers may also appoint special advisers to help them achieve their political objectives. Special advisers are appointed on Civil Service terms but, unlike civil servants, they are temporary political appointees. They are not impartial; rather, they provide ministers with political advice and will often leave office with the minister or if there is a change in government.

The role of special advisers is regulated by the *Code of Conduct for Special Advisers*, which sets out the type of work they may undertake and their relationship with the Civil Service.

4.2.3 Next Steps Agencies

Next Steps Agencies are sometimes referred to as Arm's-Length Agencies. They are used for the delivery of many government services. There are various types, operating in various ways, each having a different relationship with the political, central government.

It will commonly be the case that the relevant government department draws up the policy it wishes to pursue in a particular area and the Next Steps Agency is responsible for implementing that policy. The agency will draft a number of performance targets that are usually subject to ministerial approval. These are targets that the agency in question proposes to meet.

An example of a Next Steps Agency is the National Offender Management Service, which includes the Prison Service. This is an agency of the Ministry of Justice. In simple terms, the Secretary of State for Justice and the Minister for Prisons are responsible for setting the policy that the agency should pursue but the agency, headed by a Director-General, is responsible for the day-to-day running of the service.

The rationale behind such a system is that removing government from the day-to-day control of the service will depoliticise it and make it more efficient.

4.3 Ministerial responsibility

There are two constitutional conventions that compose the convention of ministerial responsibility and that help to ensure government in the UK is accountable: collective responsibility and individual ministerial responsibility. These two conventions are very significant and it is important that you understand them in order to understand the way in which government in the UK operates.

4.3.1 Collective responsibility

'The convention of collective responsibility means that all Ministers in the government must accept responsibility for the policies, decisions, and actions of the government, even if they did not personally develop or take them, and even if they personally disagree with them.'

(Tomkins, A., *Public Law*, 2003, Oxford: Oxford University Press)

Collective responsibility binds the individual members of the government together so that they present a united face to Parliament and the public.

It is sometimes said the convention of collective responsibility is made up of three parts: the unanimity rule, the confidentiality rule and the confidence rule.

We will look at each of these three aspects of collective responsibility in turn.

4.3.1.1 Unanimity rule

The main aspect of collective responsibility is the unanimity rule, which stipulates that all members of the Government (i.e. all ministers) must publicly support and be bound by Government policy as agreed in Cabinet or one of its committees. If a minister feels that he or she cannot publicly support Government policy then they must resign.

- For example, in 2003 Robin Cook, a member of Tony Blair's Government, decided that he could not agree with the Government's commitment to pursue military action against Iraq and so resigned from the Government.

It is thought that the principle of unanimity developed in the seventeenth and eighteenth centuries as a way of ministers presenting a united front to the monarch, who at that time would exercise personal political power and who might want to exploit divisions in Government, among ministers, for his own ends. This is no longer necessary in the modern age but unanimity has other advantages for Government.

First, unanimity is obviously politically advantageous for those in power because any public division among ministers would be used by the opposition parties to undermine the Government.

Ian Loveland states that collective responsibility preserves confidence in the Government and helps prevent unwanted economic or political consequences:

'The contemporary argument suggests the rule is needed to maintain public and business confidence in the unity and purpose of government. It is alleged that public Cabinet divisions would trigger such dire consequences as reduced investment from overseas, a run on the pound, or various other forms of economic or political instability.'

(Loveland, I., *Constitutional Law, Administrative Law, and Human Rights: A Critical Introduction*, 6th edn, 2012, Oxford: Oxford University Press)

Workpoint

What benefits do you think the principle of collective responsibility brings?

Collective responsibility has been suspended on a number of occasions.

- It was suspended by the Prime Minister, Ramsey Macdonald, in the 1931–1932 government. There were opposing views about economic policy and, in order to prevent the resignation of four members of his Cabinet, Mr Macdonald allowed them to express their views publicly.

- In 1975 Harold Wilson's Government was split as to continued membership of the EEC. The matter of the UK's continued membership was to be put to a referendum. The Prime Minister suspended the convention of collective responsibility over this matter to allow members of the Cabinet to speak on either side of the debate.

The rule is usually formulated in a way that recognises that it may be suspended. For example, the Cabinet Manual states:

'All government ministers are bound by the collective decisions of Cabinet save where it is explicitly set aside.'

(The Cabinet Office (2011) *The Cabinet Manual*)

Workpoint

In Chapter 3 I defined constitutional conventions as non-legal binding rules. Can it really be said that collective responsibility is such a binding rule if it can be set aside by the Prime Minister when it is politically convenient?

4.3.1.2 Confidentiality rule

The confidentiality rule requires that discussions among ministers, either in Cabinet or in ministerial committees, concerning the formulation of government policy, should remain confidential. The rationale underlying this convention is that ministers will speak freely, and so reach better decisions, if they are confident that their views will not be made public. Also, it would be difficult for a minister to conform to the unanimity rule – to publicly support government policy – if it became known that he or she opposed that policy during its formulation.

The current edition of the Ministerial Code – produced by the Government on taking office – states:

'The principle of collective responsibility, save where it is explicitly set aside, requires that Ministers should be able to express their views frankly in the expectation that they can argue freely in private while maintaining a united front when decisions have been reached. This in turn requires that the privacy of opinions expressed in Cabinet and Ministerial Committees, including in correspondence, should be maintained.'

(The Cabinet Office (2010) *Ministerial Code*, section 2.1)

Case:	
***Attorney-General v Jonathan Cape Ltd* [1976] QB 752**	Facts: The Government sought an injunction to prevent publication of the diaries of an ex-minister, detailing discussions within government, on the grounds that this would breach the constitutional convention of confidentiality.
	Held: The convention could give rise to a legally enforceable duty of confidentiality but that, in this particular case, the confidential nature of the diaries had been erased by the passage of time.

One may question how much the confidentiality rule is adhered to in practice. For instance, there are often leaks to the press about different opinions or positions taken by ministers in Cabinet or Government more generally.

Moreover, it is becoming more common for ministers, including the Prime Minister, to publish diaries or memoirs detailing their time in office. Ministers are free to do this so long as the publication does not contravene national security, harm relations with other nations or breach the confidentiality rule (though these diaries often describe the positions taken by different members of the Government). All ministers are required to submit such publications to the Cabinet Secretary, who will examine it and advise the author about these matters.

It is sometimes suggested that the unanimity rule and the confidentiality rule represent an ideal of collegiate government where ministers are able to agree to a position because it has been openly and freely debated with everyone having the opportunity to air their views. However, this ideal probably has little connection with the reality of modern government. The evidence is that many decisions in modern governments are taken by Prime Minister along with a small group of advisers and are presented to the other members of the Government as a fait accompli that they must either accept or resign.

4.3.1.3 Confidence rule

Collective responsibility also means that the Government should have the confidence of the House of Commons and that it should resign if this is not the case. In 1979 the Labour Government, headed by James Callaghan, resigned after losing a confidence vote in the House of Commons by one vote. This was the catalyst for the 1979 General Election that brought the Conservative Government under Margaret Thatcher to power.

This situation is now largely regulated by the Fixed-Term Parliaments Act 2011. Under section 2 of the Act, if the House of Commons passes a motion stating *'That this House has no confidence in Her Majesty's Government'* and then does not rectify this with a motion stating *'That this House has confidence in Her Majesty's Government'*, passed within 14 days of the first motion, there will be a General Election.

In addition, the Cabinet Manual states:

'The Prime Minister is expected to resign where it is clear that he or she does not have the confidence of the House of Commons and that an alternative government does have the confidence.'

(The Cabinet Office (2011) *The Cabinet Manual*)

Taken together, this means that if the Commons passes a motion of no confidence in the Government, the Prime Minister should resign to allow someone else to form a Government if it is clear that they can command the confidence of the House of Commons. Confidence in the new Government can be confirmed by a Commons vote within 14 days of the first motion of no confidence. However, if the existing Prime Minister can regain the confidence of the Commons, and this is confirmed by a Commons vote, then there need not be a change in Prime Minister.

This also means that the confidence rule is partly regulated by law (section 2 of the Fixed-Term Parliaments Act 2011) and partly by convention.

4.3.2 Individual ministerial responsibility

Ministers are individually accountable to Parliament and the public for their own behaviour and for the actions of their departments and civil servants. While this rule is easy to state in the abstract, it is often difficult to ascertain what it requires in practice. This is for a number of reasons:

- Accountability is often distinguished from responsibility, though it is not always easy to identify where one ends and the other begins.

- There is a lack of clarity about the degree to which individual ministerial responsibility governs a minister's private life.

- When there has been a breach of individual ministerial responsibility, it is not always easy to predict what the consequences will be: for instance, whether the minister should resign or not. Much here will depend on other political and non-political factors, including:
  - the degree of support given to the minister by the Prime Minister, his ministerial colleagues and party members; and
  - the way in which the media are dealing with the story – a minister who finds he or she is subject to high-profile criticism day after day will find it more difficult to remain in office than one who is not.

It is worthwhile considering three well-known examples of ministerial responsibility from the past: the Crichel Down Affair; the ministerial resignations because of the Argentine invasion of the Falkland Islands; and the lack of resignation following the breach of security at Buckingham Palace.

Crichel Down

The Crichel Down Affair arose in the 1950s. It concerned land that had been acquired by the Government for military purposes before the outbreak of the Second World War. The Ministry of Agriculture refused to resell the land back to its original owners in breach of assurances given when it was acquired. The Minister of Agriculture, Sir Thomas Dugdale, resigned because of the failings of his civil servants in the matter.

The Falklands invasion

In 1982, Argentine forces invaded the Falkland Islands. The Foreign Secretary, Lord Carrington, resigned because the Foreign Office had not sufficiently appreciated the threat posed by Argentina.

Palace security

In 1982, an intruder managed to evade security at Buckingham Palace and enter the Queen's bedroom while she was there. William Whitelaw considered resigning as Home Secretary but was persuaded not to by the Prime Minister, Margaret Thatcher.

These examples illustrate some of the uncertainty of individual ministerial responsibility. It is perhaps reasonable that Whitelaw did not resign over the breach of palace security because he was probably not directly at fault. Yet, in 1954, Dugdale felt the need to resign even though he was unaware of the actions of his civil servants with regard to Crichel Down. Today, as we shall see, ministers are not expected to resign over matters for which they are not personally to blame.

The current advice with regard to ministers' responsibility is given in the Ministerial Code; among other things, the Code states that individual ministerial responsibility requires ministers to:

- be accountable to Parliament for the policies, actions and decisions of their department and of any Next Steps Agencies;

- be truthful and as open as possible with Parliament and the public;

- ensure that no conflict arises between their public duties and private interests.

What is meant by accountability? We can take guidance from the definition given by the Public Service Committee:

'Ministers owe a fundamental duty to account to Parliament. This has, essentially, two meanings. First, that the executive is obliged to give an account – to provide full information about and explain its actions in

Parliament so that they are subject to proper democratic scrutiny.... Second, a Minister's duty to account to Parliament means that the executive is liable to be held to account: it must respond to concerns and criticisms raised in Parliament about its actions because Members of Parliament are democratically-elected representatives of the people. A Minister's effective performance of his functions depends on his having the confidence of the House of Commons (or the House of Lords, for those Ministers who sit in the upper House). A Minister has to conduct himself, and direct the work of his department in a manner likely to ensure that he retains the confidence both of his own party and of the House.'

(Public Service Committee, *Ministerial Accountability and Responsibility* (1995–1996 HC 313) para. 32)

That is, accountability means that ministers should explain, defend and give information about the actions of their departments. It also means that they are expected to respond to concerns raised by Parliament and conduct themselves in a way that retains the confidence of Parliament.

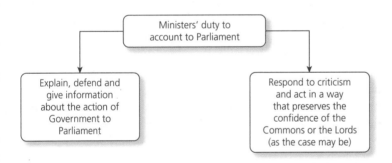

Accountability to Parliament primarily occurs in two ways.

a) *In the Chambers of the House of Commons and the House of Lords*

Ministers are expected to explain and defend the Government's actions on the floor of each House of Parliament. One of the main ways in which this will occur is during ministerial question time. Most readers will be aware of Prime Minister's Question Time where, on Wednesdays, the Prime Minister answers questions in the House of Commons about the Government's actions or decisions. Less well known is the fact that there is also a question time for each government department whereby the ministers of that department answer questions in Parliament about the policies and actions of their department.

Ministers will also explain and defend Government policies during debates and the passing of legislation.

b) *Select committees*

The work of select committees takes place outside of the chambers of the Commons and the Lords. There are different types of select committees, including:

1) ad hoc select committees, which may investigate and report on particular issues; these are less common nowadays;

2) regular or permanent select committees, such as the Public Accounts Committee, which regularly deal with specific matters;

3) departmental select committees, which are creatures of the House of Commons and which investigate the work undertaken by particular government departments.

Select committees can question ministers and civil servants in more depth than would otherwise be possible. They may also take evidence from other interest groups including academics, business representatives and members of the public.

Departmental select committees issue annual and special reports that may be debated in the House of Commons.

In addition to Parliament, ministers are often accountable to the public more directly via the news media. The importance of the press in holding the government to account is widely recognised as essential to a healthy democracy and there are many instances where the press has uncovered governmental or official wrongdoing.

Workpoint

Can you think of any instances where the press has been instrumental in uncovering governmental or official wrongdoing?

4.3.2.1 Accountability or responsibility?

A distinction is often drawn between *accountability* and *responsibility*.

• Accountability is taken to mean that ministers are under a duty to explain and defend their decisions or actions and those of their department and its agencies.

• Responsibility is taken to mean those things for which the minister may personally take credit or blame.

It will be seen that according to this, the obligation of accountability is much wider than that of responsibility.

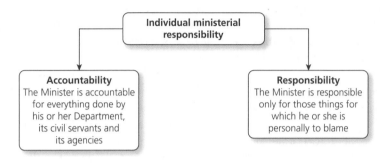

This division between responsibility and accountability seems appropriate given the size and complexity of modern government. It would not seem reasonable to expect a minister to personally take the blame for things they did not know about and could not possibly have known about.

However, it is not possible to draw an absolute distinction between the things for which the minister is responsible and one for which he or she is accountable. This has been recognised by the Public Service Committee:

'It is not possible absolutely to distinguish an area in which a Minister is personally responsible, and liable to take blame, from one in which he is constitutionally accountable. Ministerial responsibility is not composed of two elements with a clear break between the two. Ministers have an obligation to Parliament which consists in ensuring that government explains its actions. Ministers also have an obligation to respond to criticism made in Parliament in a way that seems likely to satisfy it – which may include, if necessary, resignation.'

(Public Service Committee, *Ministerial Accountability and Responsibility*, 1995–1996 HC 313, para 21)

For example, if there were an escape of prisoners from a particular prison the relevant minister might argue that, while they are under a duty to account for what has gone wrong, they are not responsible for the day-to-day running of prisons. Yet the distinction between accountability and responsibility may be difficult to maintain if it became apparent that the escape is the direct result of the minister's policies, perhaps because he or she has underfunded the Prison Service with the result that individual prison governors cannot adequately staff their institutions.

4.3.2.2 Personal issues

One question is whether issues in a minister's personal life are relevant to individual ministerial responsibility. The general view is that they are not. So, for instance, if a minister is found to be having an extramarital affair, then this is generally considered to be a private matter that does not affect the minister's public role.

There may be exceptions to this where, for example, a minister's private conduct gives rise to a conflict with their public duties or is an issue of national security (perhaps because of a risk of blackmail).

Moreover, a minister may be forced to resign as a result of private conduct if it becomes embarrassing for the Government – though this might be thought to be a matter of political expedience rather than demanded by ministerial responsibility.

4.3.2.3 The purpose of individual ministerial responsibility

There are a number of rationales for individual ministerial responsibility, including:

- It is part of a healthy democracy that those in government explain and defend their decisions to the public via Parliament and, if necessary, that they take remedial action in response to valid criticisms.

- It helps to ensure fitness for public office by making sure that ministers are trustworthy, honest, incorruptible and act with integrity.

- It helps to maintain the impartiality of the Civil Service by making ministers, rather than civil servants, politically accountable for the actions of government.

4.3.3 Ministerial responsibility: overview

Diagrammatically, and as a whole, ministerial responsibility looks like this:

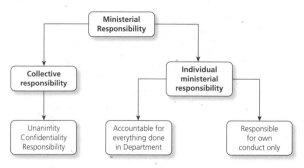

Perhaps the most important question with regard to ministerial responsibility – both collective and individual – is whether the systems that we have in place are as effective as they could be to ensure that we have accountable and responsible government. This is something over which people may legitimately disagree. However, we should note the following.

- Parliament's ability to hold the Government to account may be limited by a lack of time and resources. It may also be hampered by the fact that Parliament is a body largely controlled by the Government (because the Government has a majority of support in the House of Commons).

- The distinction between accountability and responsibility is not always clear and this lack of clarity may be used by ministers to escape responsibility even when they are culpable.

- The use of Next Steps Agencies to deliver some government services can mean that, with respect to those services, it is not easy to clearly distinguish the matters for which a minister should be held responsible from those for which he or she is merely accountable.

Checkpoint – Responsible government and accountability

Item on checklist:	Done!
I can explain why it is desirable to have accountable government.	
I can explain why the Government will usually have the support of the majority of MPs in the House of Commons.	
I can give a brief description of the Cabinet.	
I can describe the Civil Service including what is meant when it is said that the Civil Service is the impartial, permanent part of government.	
I know what Next Steps Agencies are.	
With regard to collective responsibility, I can describe: • the unanimity rule • the confidentiality rule • the confidence rule.	

Checkpoint – Responsible government and accountability

Item on checklist:	Done!
I know the meaning of accountability and can explain the difference between accountability and responsibility.	
I can explain the ways in which Parliament holds the Government to account.	
I can explain why the ways in which the Government is held to account may be less than fully effective.	

Research Point

Review the newspapers over the past 18 months or so. Have there been any ministerial resignations? Did those resignations involve issues of collective or individual responsibility and, if so, what were they?

Research Point

Read the following article: Brazier, R. 'It Is a Constitutional Issue: Fitness for Ministerial Office in the 1990s' [1994] *Public Law* 431. What solutions does Brazier suggest to make sure that ministers are fit for office? Are his solutions workable?

Research Point

Watch a video of the famous 1997 interview of the then Home Secretary Michael Howard by Jeremy Paxman (you should be able to find this on the Internet using a search engine).
Why do you think Mr Howard had such an awkward time in the interview? What issues of ministerial responsibility were at issue?

Potential exam question

How do the conventions of collective responsibility and individual ministerial responsibility attempt to secure accountable government in the UK?

Chapter 5
Separation of powers and judicial independence

In this chapter you will learn about:

- the meaning and rationale of the separation of powers principle;

- the division of the powers of state into three functions: the executive function, the legislative function and the judicial function;

- the degree to which the UK adheres to the separation of powers principle;

- the meaning and rationale of judicial independence;

- the ways in which the independence of the judiciary is secured in the UK.

5.1 Separation of powers: overview

It is considered desirable that the powers of government should be divided into three separate functions – the executive function, the legislative function and the judicial function – and that these three functions are exercised by different bodies: the executive, the legislature and the judiciary.

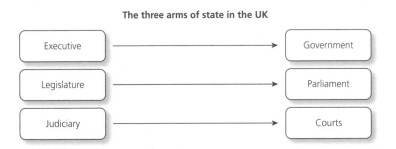

The three arms of state in the UK

Executive	→ Government
Legislature	→ Parliament
Judiciary	→ Courts

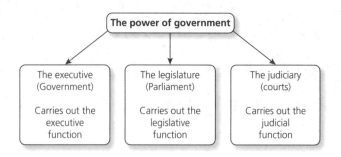

Separation of powers is a principle that a legal/political system will meet to a greater or lesser extent. A common question asked of students on this topic is the degree to which the UK adheres to the principle of separation of powers. We will look at how such a question may be answered, below. First, we will look at the rationale underlying the principle.

5.2 The rationale underlying separation of powers

The development of the separation of powers principle in the form that we know it is accredited to the French philosopher Baron de Montesquieu (1689–1755), who built on the work of the earlier English philosopher John Locke (1632–1704).

Workpoint

Read the two quotations from Locke and Montesquieu, below. Can you identify why they believe it is desirable for the power of government to be divided?

'It may be too great a temptation to human frailty, apt to grasp at power, for the same persons who have the power of making laws, to have also in their hands the power to execute them, whereby they may exempt themselves from obedience to the laws they make, and suit the law, both in its making and execution, to their own private advantage.'
(Locke, J., *Second Treatise of Civil Government*, 1690, chapter XII)

'When the Legislative Power is united with the Executive Power in the same person or body of magistrates, there is no liberty because it is to be feared that the same Monarch or the same Senate will make tyrannical

laws in order to execute them tyrannically. There is no liberty if the Judicial Power is not separated from the Legislative Power and from the Executive Power. If it were joined with the Legislative Power, the power over the life and liberty of citizens would be arbitrary, because the judge would be Legislator. If it were joined to the Executive Power, the Judge would have the strength of an oppressor. All would be lost if the same man, or the same body of chief citizens, or the nobility, or the people, exercised these three powers, that of making laws, that of executing public decisions, and that of judging the crimes or the disputes of private persons.'

(Montesquieu, C., *De l'Espirit des Lois*, 2nd edn, 1748, book XI, chapter VI)

Locke seems to imagine that if the power of the state were concentrated in the same people, they would be tempted to make and implement law for their own advantage and to exempt themselves from obedience to it.

Montesquieu's concern is that if the three functions of government were concentrated in the same body, then there would be a temptation towards tyranny and oppression where the power exercised over citizens would be arbitrary.

Separation means the three arms of government can act as a check on each other. For instance, in the UK:

- the executive can gather taxes only if they are given the power to do so by the legislature and any imposition of taxes can be tested in the courts;

- the courts can only apply law that has been approved explicitly (by enacting legislation) or implicitly (by not enacting legislation to change the common law) by the legislature;

- any legislation enacted by the legislature relies on the executive to implement it and the courts to interpret and apply it.

There is something inherent in the above that separation of powers is not simply about separation. Each of the three arms of state – executive, legislature and judiciary – are expected to act as a check on the other two so that none of the three arms of state are able to abuse their powers. This is sometimes referred to as the requirement that there should be checks and balances.

5.3 Separation of powers in the UK

Consider the following two statements, the first from Lord Diplock (a very senior judge) and the second from Stanley de Smith and Rodney Brazier (distinguished and well-respected academics):

Lord Diplock:

'it cannot be too strongly emphasised that the British constitution, though largely unwritten, is firmly based upon the separation of powers.'
(*Duport Steels Ltd v Sirs* [1980] 1 WLR 142, 157)

De Smith and Brazier:

'No writer of repute would claim that it [separation of powers] is a central feature of the modern British Constitution.'
(de Smith, S. and Brazier, R., *Constitutional and Administrative Law*, 8th edn, 1998, London: Penguin)

We can instantly see that there is a lack of agreement about whether the UK adheres to the separation of powers principle. Given this, we need to find our own answer to the question and, in doing this, it is useful to have a more detailed account of what separation requires.

A good starting point here is to refer to the following definition of separation of powers given by Bradley and Ewing:

'The concept of "separation" may mean at least three different things:

a) that the same persons should not form part of more than one of the three branches of the state, for example, that ministers (being members of the executive) should not sit in Parliament;

b) that one branch of the state should not control or intervene in the work of another, for example, that the executive should not interfere in judicial decisions;

c) that one branch should not exercise the functions of another, for example, that ministers should not have judicial powers.'

(Bradley, A.W. and Ewing, K.D., *Constitutional and Administrative Law*, 15th edn, 2011, London: Longman)

That is, the separation of powers has three different aspects to do with personnel, control and functions.

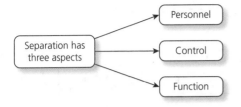

We can then examine the position of the UK in each of these three categories. Before that, we should be certain we understand what they mean.

• *Personnel*

The ideal position is where there are three separate bodies – an executive, a legislature and a judiciary – and that no one is a member of more than one body.

The absolute antithesis of the ideal position is where one body, or even one person, composes the executive, the legislative and the judiciary.

• *Control*

This is fairly obvious: one of the powers should not control another either *de jure* (in law) or de facto (in fact).

• *Functions*

The third aspect of the separation of the powers is that no arm of state should exercise a function that more properly belongs to one of the others.

We can use these three aspects of separation as a framework to help us to assess whether there are any infringements of separation in respect of each.

Workpoint

Bradley and Ewing also write: *'the complete separation of powers is possible neither in theory or in practice'* (Bradley, A.W. and Ewing, K.D., *Constitutional and Administrative Law*, 15th edn, 2011, London: Longman).
Why do you think complete separation is not possible? Would complete separation ever be desirable?

5.3.1 Infringement in terms of personnel

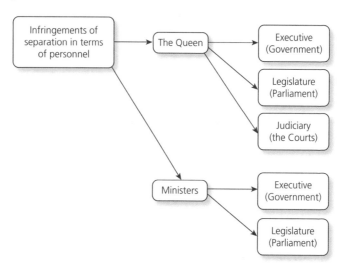

The Queen

Nominally, the Queen is a member of all three arms of state.

- The Queen is the legal head of Government – it is Her Majesty's Government.

- Parliament is made up of the Queen, the House of Commons and the House of Lords – indeed, in formal terms Parliament is sometimes referred to as 'The Queen in Parliament'.

- The Queen is part of the courts system – the courts are the Queen's Courts; judges derive their authority from the Queen and exercise their function in her name; she is the Fount (source) of all Justice.

So, on the face of it, the monarch seems to significantly infringe the principle of separation. However, the reality is different and the Queen's role in each of the three arms of state is largely ceremonial and tightly circumscribed by constitutional convention; she does not exercise real political power.

- Her executive power is exercised on her behalf by her ministers.

- Her legislative power (mostly, assenting to legislation passed by the Commons and the Lords) is not exercised personally and, as we saw in Chapter 3, is governed by constitutional convention (see Section 3.2).

- Justice may be exercised in the Queen's name but not by her and she takes no part in the judicial process.

In short, when answering a question about separation of powers in the UK, it is appropriate to mention the position of the Queen but you should also stress that her role is largely ceremonial with the result that any infringement of separation is in reality inconsequential.

Ministers

The position of ministers is a significant infringement of the separation of powers principle. As we have seen in Chapters 3 and 4, it is a constitutional convention that all ministers must be a member of either the House of Commons or the House of Lords. This means that ministers are members of both the executive and the legislature, thereby breaching the principle of separation.

If you find yourself answering a question about separation of powers in the UK, there is an opportunity here to make a relatively sophisticated point about the position of ministers. That is, the conventional rule that requires ministers to belong to Parliament is thought necessary because it enables Parliament to directly hold the Government to account (see Chapter 4). Thus, it could be argued that, in the UK, absolute adherence to one principle – separation of powers – has been sacrificed to achieve another – direct accountability of Government to Parliament.

Historical infringements

It is worth noting that there were, until recently, two other significant infringements of separation with regard to personnel: the role of the Lord Chancellor; and Law Lords sitting in the Appellate Committee of the House of Lords.

The Lord Chancellor

Until 2005, the Lord Chancellor was an active member of all three arms of state.

- He was (and still is) a member of the executive as a senior Cabinet minister.

- He was the head of the judiciary and would sit as a judge.

- He was the Speaker of the House of Lords, i.e. a member of the legislature.

His position was altered by the Constitutional Reform Act 2005. He is no longer part of the judiciary and will not sit as a judge. Also, he does not act as the Speaker of the House of Lords – the Lords now elect their own speaker.

In fact, the Lord Chancellor need not be a member of the House of Lords; he can be a member of the Commons or the Lords.

The current position of the Lord Chancellor (who is also now the Secretary of State for Justice) is no different from any other minister: he is a member of the executive and the legislature.

Law Lords

Until 2009, the final court of appeal for civil cases in England, Wales and Northern Ireland, and for all UK criminal cases, was a committee of the House of Lords: the Appellate Committee of the House of Lords. The judges who sat in this court, Lords of Appeal in Ordinary (Law Lords), were therefore members of the judiciary and, because they were peers, members of the legislature.

In 2009, the relevant provisions of the Constitutional Reform Act 2005 came into effect and the judicial functions of the House of Lords were transferred to a new Supreme Court of the United Kingdom. The first Justices of this new court were the former Law Lords, though they are prohibited from sitting as peers in the House of Lords until they retire as Justices. Future Justices of the Supreme Court will not be peers entitled to sit in the House of Lords, though they will be given the title 'Lord' or 'Lady'.

Note: You should be clear that the situation with regard to the Lord Chancellor and Law Lords has changed. An understanding of the situation will help you appreciate how separation of powers has become more of a feature of the UK constitution but you should be careful not to confuse the historical position with the current one.

5.3.2 Infringement in terms of control

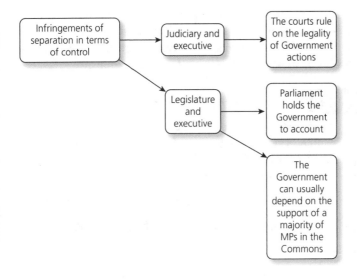

The judiciary and the executive
The courts will rule on the legality of Government action in many cases and so it may be said that the judiciary are exercising some control over the executive. However, the control exercised is considered perfectly legitimate – the courts are simply ensuring that the Government acts lawfully – and, indeed, may be said to be part of the checks and balances aspect of separation of powers.

The executive and the legislature
A more questionable issue of control exists with the relationship between Government and Parliament. We saw in Chapter 4 that one of the roles of Parliament is to hold the Government to account, to require the Government to explain and defend its actions. Indeed, we also saw that the Government needs the support of the majority in the House of Commons to remain in office (see Section 4.3.1.3). As with the courts, this seems legitimate in separation of powers terms: it represents a check by the legislature on executive power.

However, we also saw in Chapter 4 that, because the Government will have the support of a majority of MPs, it is able to exercise a great deal of control over the House of Commons. This is a more questionable control of one arm of state by another because it has implications for the ability of Parliament to carry out its functions independently from Government.

We should note here that the ability of the Government to dominate the House of Commons is limited by s 2 of the House of Commons Disqualification Act 1975, which limits the number of ministers in the Commons to 95. However, we should also note that there will be 20 to 30 Parliamentary Private Secretaries in addition to this 95 who are also obliged to vote with the Government.

> **Definition**
>
> **Parliamentary Private Secretaries:** MPs who act as ministerial aides and whose role involves keeping the minister abreast of opinion in the House of Commons; they are not formally part of the government.

5.3.3 Infringement in terms of function

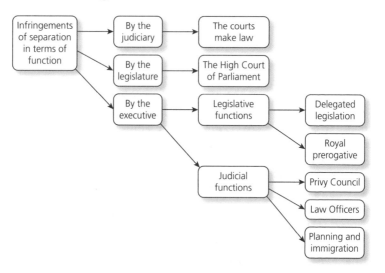

In order to evaluate whether there is any infringement of the separation principle in terms of function, it will be useful to have a clearer picture of what the three functions of state are.

- *The executive function*

  In brief, the executive is concerned with the day-to-day administration of the state. In particular, the role of the executive includes:
  - maintenance of order and security (this is sometimes claimed to be the primary purpose of government);
  - formation of policy;

- initiating legislation – that is, offering proposed legislation to the legislature;
- implementation of legislation – that is, once legislation has been enacted, it is the executive's job to put it into effect;
- responsibility for the day-to-day administration and control of public services such as the police, the welfare state, the armed forces;
- responsibility for the external relations of the state – e.g. foreign policy, treaties, making peace and war;
- setting the taxing and spending plans of Government.

- *The legislative function*

  The job of the legislature is to legislate: to enact laws.

- *The judicial function*

  The role of the judiciary is to resolve legal disputes and, in doing so, determine what the law requires in any particular situation.

The three functions

Executive	Legislative	Judicial
• order and security • policy • initiate legislation • execute laws • foreign affairs • administration • spending and tax	• enact laws	• resolve legal disputes

Infringements by the judiciary
Judges make law, both in the development of the common law and the application of statute law to new situations. One could therefore argue that judges are carrying out a function that more properly belongs to the legislature. However, I suggest that the creation of law is an unavoidable part of the judicial function.

So, it is worth noting that there is some possible infringement by the courts here but it is also worth making the point that this is an inevitable corollary of the role of the courts.

Infringements by the legislature
It is sometimes suggested that Parliament has a residual power as a court; indeed, it is sometimes known as the High Court of Parliament. This, though, is not part of its day-to-day activities and the extent of its jurisdiction is not entirely certain.

Parliament certainly has the power to deal with its own internal affairs (though whether this is an example of a judicial function is debatable). It also seems to have the power to compel witnesses to appear before its committees and to deal with any contempt of Parliament. It does not, though, appear to have the power to deal with ordinary crimes committed by members of either House.

Having said that, it is sometimes suggested that Parliament may have a power of impeachment whereby a person may be prosecuted and tried for a crime by the two Houses. If it does exist, this power is likely to be exercised only with regard to ministers. In fact, there was an attempt by some MPs to impeach the then Prime Minister, Tony Blair, in 2004. This failed because of a lack of support. It seems likely that this power of impeachment is obsolete. In any case, any conviction would probably be in breach of the right to a fair trial guaranteed by the European Convention on Human Rights.

Historically, of course, the Appellate Committee of the House of Lords was the final court of appeal for many matters. However, this role is now undertaken by the Supreme Court of the UK (see Section 5.3.1 above).

Infringements by the executive
The Government in the UK exercises some legislative and judicial functions.

• *Legislative functions undertaken by the executive*
    The Government has the power to create law in two ways.
    a) Delegated legislation
        Ministers, local authorities and public bodies are often given power by an Act of Parliament to create secondary legislation.
        Ministers may also be given power by a clause in an Act of Parliament to amend Acts of Parliament; such a clause is known as a Henry VIII (Henry the Eighth) clause.
    b) The royal prerogative
        Ministers will sometimes use the residual common law prerogative power of the monarch to create law. This will take place as an Order in Council, i.e. an order of the Privy Council.

Definition

The Privy Council: Historically an advisory body to the monarch; its role is now largely to give formal effect to acts undertaken using statutory or prerogative powers, though it also has a judicial function.

Definition

> **Primary and secondary legislation:** Primary legislation refers primarily to Acts of Parliament, though it also includes some legislation created using the royal prerogative; secondary legislation refers to legislation created by some lesser body.

- Judicial functions undertaken by the executive

There are three possible infringements of separation here concerning the Privy Council, the Law Officers and certain planning and immigration decisions.

   a) The Judicial Committee of the Privy Council

   The Judicial Committee of the Privy Council is the final court of appeal for UK overseas territories, Crown Dependencies and some former colonies of the UK.

   Because the Privy Council is formally part of the executive, the exercise of judicial functions infringes the principle of separation. However, this infringement is formal only because the judges of the Judicial Committee are the Justices of the Supreme Court and they act independently of Government.

   b) UK Law Officers

   The Law Officers are the Attorney General (who is also the Advocate General for Northern Ireland), the Solicitor General and the Advocate General for Scotland. Their main function is to advise the Government on legal matters. However, it is sometimes said that they have a quasi-judicial role, including:
   - granting consent to bring certain types of prosecution;
   - referring unduly lenient sentences to the Court of Appeal;
   - referring points of law to the Court of Appeal after acquittal in criminal cases;
   - acting to restrain vexatious litigants.

   c) Certain planning and immigration decisions

   Ministers have the power to make the final decision on some large planning applications or in some immigration cases, matters which are sometimes said to be judicial in nature.

   However, with regard to these decisions by ministers and the functions of the Law Officers, it is difficult to see how they can definitely be classified as judicial, or even quasi-judicial, in nature.

Indeed, Bradley and Ewing write on this point:

'There is no sharp distinction between decisions which should be entrusted to courts and tribunals on the one hand, and those which should be entrusted to administrative authorities on the other.'

(Bradley, A.W. and Ewing, K.D., *Constitutional and Administrative Law*, 15th edn, 2011, London: Longman)

It is worth noting that the Home Secretary did have power to set the tariff (the minimum sentence) to be served by those given a life sentence. She no longer has this power; it was removed by the Criminal Justice and Courts Service Act 2000 (with regard to juveniles) and the Criminal Justice Act 2003 (with regard to adults).

Workpoint

On the following table, detail the infringements of separation of power in the UK by the three arms of state in terms of personnel, control and functions.

	Personnel	Control	Functions
Executive (Government)			
Legislature (Parliament)			
Judiciary (Courts)			

Checkpoint – Separation of powers

Item on checklist:	Done!
I can name the three arms of government.	
I can name the bodies that represent these three arms in the UK.	
I can explain the rationale underpinning the principle of separation of powers.	
I can give an account of: • the executive function • the legislative function • the judicial function.	
I can list possible infringements of the principle of separation in the UK in terms of: • personnel • control • function.	

5.4 The independence of the judiciary

'There are countries in the world where all judicial decisions find favour with the government, but they are not places where one would wish to live.'

(Lord Bingham, 'The Rule of Law' [2007] CLJ 67)

> **Workpoint**
>
> Read the above quotation. Why would one not want to live in a country where all judicial decisions find favour with the government?

5.4.1 Judicial independence: overview

It is considered desirable that the judiciary should be independent. This means at least two things: freedom from bias and freedom from external control.

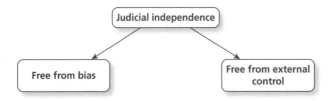

Free from bias
It is important that judges decide cases impartially, according to their merits and the law, rather than being influenced by personal prejudices or a bias towards one litigant over another.

This is recognised by the current Lord Chief Justice, Sir Igor Judge:

'The independence of the judiciary is something which is precious to every single member of the community. You must be able to go into court and know that the person sitting in judgment is neutral – not on one side or the other – coldly applying the law that applies to your case.'

(Sixth Report of the House of Lords Select Committee on the Constitution, *Relations Between the Executive, the Judiciary and Parliament* (2007 HL 151))

This is an issue of fairness. We want the courts to decide cases in a manner that is openly fair and just.

Case:	
R v Sussex Justices, ex parte McCarthy [1924] 1 KB 256	Lord Hewart CJ: *'[It] is of fundamental importance that justice should not only be done, but should manifestly and undoubtedly be seen to be done.'*

Free from external control

Judges should be able to exercise their role free from external pressures, particularly pressure from the Government.

It is important to realise that the Government is one of the parties in many cases before the courts:

• Criminal prosecutions are, except for a few private prosecutions, brought by the Government in the name of the Crown. This is reflected in their name: R v Smith (i.e. the Crown (or the Queen) against Smith).

• In many cases, the courts are ruling on the legality of judicial action (see Chapters 10 and 11 on judicial review).

In cases such as these, the Government has a vested interest in the case being decided one way rather than another.

Even where the Government is not one of the parties to a case, the decision may have implications for the Government in terms of its policies or civil liabilities.

Given these potential vested interests on the part of the Government, and the desirability of cases being decided impartially, it is important that judges are protected from governmental pressure.

5.4.2 Judicial independence in the UK

Judicial independence (in terms of insulation from external pressure) in the UK is secured in the following ways:

- *Statutory guarantee*

  Section 3 of the Constitutional Reform Act 2005 guarantees the independence of the judiciary. In particular, s 3(1) and (5) puts an obligation on the Lord Chancellor and other ministers to uphold judicial independence and to refrain from attempting to influence judicial decisions through any special access they might have.

  Section 3 Guarantee of continued judicial independence

  1) *The Lord Chancellor, other Ministers of the Crown and all with responsibility for matters relating to the judiciary or otherwise to the administration of justice must uphold the continued independence of the judiciary.*

     . . .

  5) *The Lord Chancellor and other Ministers of the Crown must not seek to influence particular judicial decisions through any special access to the judiciary.*

- *Protection from arbitrary removal from office*

  Judicial independence might be under threat if the Government were able to sack judges arbitrarily. Because of this, judges are given security of tenure.
  - Judges in the Crown Court, High Court, Court of Appeal and the Supreme Court remain in office during good behaviour and may

only be removed on an address to the monarch from both Houses of Parliament, i.e. if both Houses vote to remove a judge. This is provided for by s 33 of the Constitutional Reform Act 2005 (for Justices of the Supreme Court) and s 11 of the Senior Courts Act 1981 (for judges in the other courts).

- Other judges may be removed by the Lord Chancellor for incapacity or misbehaviour but only with the agreement of the Lord Chief Justice (s 17(4) Courts Act 1971).
- Magistrates may be removed by the Lord Chancellor with the agreement of the Lord Chief Justice for incapacity, misbehaviour, incompetence or failure to properly exercise their functions (s 11 Courts Act 2003).

- *Protection of salary*

The independence of judges could also be under threat if their salaries could be reduced for political reasons. For this reason, their salaries are paid out of the Consolidated Fund, which is approved without parliamentary debate.

There is provision for the Lord Chancellor to increase judicial salaries, which might be necessary in a period of rapid inflation, but not to decrease them.

- *Independent appointments system*

The procedure by which judges are appointed is much more transparent and open than it once was.

- Most judicial appointments follow the recommendation of a candidate to the Lord Chancellor by the Judicial Appointments Commission.
- For Justices of the Supreme Court, a recommendation is made to the Prime Minister by a Selection Commission consisting of:
  - President of the Supreme Court (unless this is the vacant office);
  - Deputy President of the Supreme Court (unless this is the vacant office);
  - One member of the Judicial Appointments Commission;
  - One member of the Judicial Appointments Commission for Scotland.

- *Judges are not asked to comment on Government policy*

The Cabinet Manual states:

'[P]rinciples of judicial independence mean that the judiciary should not be asked to comment on the merits of proposed government policy,

and individual judicial office-holders should not be asked to comment on matters that may then require the judge to disqualify him or herself in subsequent legislation.'

(The Cabinet Office (2011) *The Cabinet Manual*)

• *The* sub judice *rule*

Generally speaking, parliamentarians will refrain from discussing the merits of cases being tried, or about to be tried, by the courts. The rationale underlying the rule is to prevent current cases being subjected to political pressure.

Checkpoint – The independence of the judiciary

Item on checklist:	Done!
I can explain why judicial independence is important.	
I understand the potential threats to judicial independence.	
I can explain the ways in which judicial independence is secured in the UK.	

Research Point

I said above that the job of the legislature is to legislate. Can you discover the other functions undertaken by the UK Parliament?

Research Point

Read the journal article, Barendt, E. 'Separation of Powers and Constitutional Government' [1995] *Public Law* 599. The author distinguishes between pure and partial separation of powers.
   Can you identify the differences between these two categories? Which category does he suggest the UK falls into?

Research Point

Look at the provisions of the Constitutional Reform Act 2005. Which sections do you think are concerned with enhancing or protecting separation of powers and the independence of the judiciary?

Research Point

Read pp. 91–92 of Bingham, T., *The Rule of Law*, 2010, London: Allen Lane.
Which legislation does Lord Bingham credit with first protecting judges against arbitrary removal by government? What does he claim judges should be independent of? What does he claim would be a threat to judicial independence?

Potential exam question

In what ways does the UK fail to meet the principle of separation of powers?

Chapter 6

Parliament and supremacy

Parliamentary supremacy is the fundamental doctrine of the UK constitution but whether it still exists as traditionally conceived is not clear. It is almost certain that you will be assessed on this topic and so it is worthwhile spending some time examining the traditional view of parliamentary supremacy and some possible qualifications of it.

In this chapter you will learn about:

• the composition of Parliament;

• the legislative process;

• the traditional view of parliamentary supremacy;

• some possible qualifications of the traditional view.

6.1 Parliament

Parliament is made up of three bodies:

• the House of Commons

• the House of Lords

• the monarch.

This composition is reflected in its more formal name: the Queen in Parliament.

Parliament		
The Queen	House of Commons	House of Lords
	• 650 directly elected MPs	• 650 life peers • 92 hereditary peers • 26 Bishops

Note: At the time of writing there are plans to reform the composition of both Houses: to reduce the number of MPs in the House of Commons and to make the House of Lords partly elected and partly appointed.

6.2 Types of legislation

Definition

Bill: The name given to proposed legislation before it is passed by Parliament.

Act: The name given to legislation that has passed all its legislative stages.

Types of legislation	
Public Bills	Legislation that applies to the public generally.
Private Bills	Legislation that applies to particular individuals or organisations.
Hybrid Bills	Legislation that applies generally but that affects individuals or organisations in a particular way.
Government Bills	Legislation initiated by the Government.
Private Members' Bills	Legislation initiated by an MP or peer (not to be confused with a Private Bill).
Money Bills	Legislation concerned wholly with financial matters.
Consolidation Bills	Legislation bringing disparate legislation together into one consolidating Bill.

6.3 The legislative process

Most legislation enacted by Parliament is initiated by the Government. There are facilities for other MPs or peers to draft and introduce their own legislation.

Legislation can begin in either House but by convention some types of legislation will always begin in one House rather than another.

- For example, Money Bills, concerned with the spending or raising of revenue, mostly begin in the House of Commons.

Legislation will go through the same legislative stages whether it starts in the Commons or the Lords.

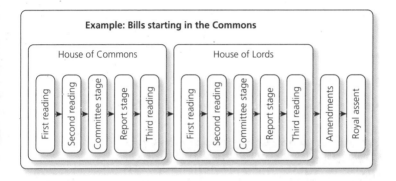

The amendments stage is where one House agrees to the amendments inserted into the legislation by the other House. Where there is no agreement on amendments, a period of negotiation between the two Houses will take place. During this time the Bill may pass from House to House, a process that is colloquially referred to as 'ping-pong'.

We can see from the above that a Bill becomes an Act when it is passed by the Commons, the Lords and receives royal assent. The exception to this is where an Act is passed using the procedure under the Parliament Acts.

6.3.1 The Parliament Acts 1911 and 1949

The Parliament Act 1911 was amended by the Parliament Act 1949 and they are commonly referred to together as the Parliament Acts 1911 and 1949. They allow legislation to be passed by the Commons alone and receive royal assent without the agreement of the House of Lords.

- Money Bills: the House of Lords cannot reject Money Bills, they can only delay them for one month. A Money Bill sent to the Lords within one month of the end of a parliamentary session, which is not passed without amendment, may be sent for royal assent.

- Non-money Bills may be delayed by the Lords for a year over two parliamentary sessions.

> **Definition**
>
> **Parliamentary session:** The parliamentary year, beginning with the State Opening of Parliament.

Exclusions from the Parliament Acts

The following may not be enacted using the Parliament Acts:

- Private Bills;

- Bills originating in the House of Lords;

- Bills extending the life of Parliament beyond five years.

Checkpoint – The composition of Parliament and the legislative process

Item on checklist:	Done!
I know the three bodies that make up Parliament and can give an account of their composition.	
I can give an account of how a Bill becomes an Act.	
I can explain the legislative process under the Parliament Acts 1911 and 1949 and how this differs from the normal legislative process.	

6.4 Parliamentary supremacy: the traditional approach

Parliamentary supremacy is also known as parliamentary sovereignty. Briefly, it is the rule that Parliament may enact any law whatsoever.

Dicey writes:

'The principle of parliamentary sovereignty means neither more nor less than this: namely, that Parliament ... has ... the right to make or unmake any law whatever; and, further, that no person or body is recognised by the law of England as having a right to override or set aside the legislation of Parliament ... The same principle looked from its negative side, may be thus stated: there is no person or body of persons who can ... make rules which override or derogate from an Act of Parliament, or

which (to express the same thing in other words) will be enforced by the courts in contravention of an Act of Parliament.'

(Dicey, A.V., Introduction to the Study of the Law of the Constitution 10th edn, 1959, London: Macmillan [1898])

The principle that the legislature can enact any law whatsoever is unusual. While it can be found in other countries (New Zealand, for example), in most countries the courts may rule legislation invalid if it breaches, say, limits imposed by the constitution.

It is useful to think of parliamentary supremacy as comprising four interrelated rules.

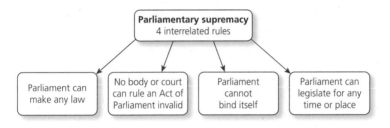

6.4.1 Parliament can make any law

There are no legal restrictions on the legislative competence of Parliament.

Case:	
Madzimbamuto v Lardner-Burke [1969] 1 AC 645	Lord Reid: *'It is often said that it would be unconstitutional for the UK Parliament to do certain things, meaning that the moral, political and other reasons against doing them are so strong that most people would regard it as highly improper if Parliament did those things. But that does not mean that it is beyond the power of Parliament to do such things. If Parliament chose to do any of them the courts would not hold the Act of Parliament invalid.'*

6.4.2 No body or court of law can rule an Act of Parliament invalid

The courts have no jurisdiction to rule an Act of Parliament invalid on any grounds.

Cases:	
Edinburgh and Dalkeith Railway Co. v Wauchope (1842) 8 Cl & F 710	Facts: Wauchope argued that the correct procedure had not been followed when passing an Act of Parliament. Lord Campbell: *'All that a court of justice can do is to look to the Parliamentary Roll: if from that it should appear that a Bill has passed both Houses and received royal assent, no court of justice can inquire into the mode in which it was introduced into Parliament, nor what was done previous to its introduction, or what passed in Parliament during its progress.'*
Lee v Bude & Torrington Junction Railway Company (1871) LR 6 CP 576	Facts: Lee complained that an Act of Parliament had been obtained fraudulently. Willes J: *'If an Act of Parliament has been obtained improperly, it is for the legislature to correct it by repealing it; but so long as it exists in law, the courts are bound to obey it.'*
British Railways Board v Pickin [1974] AC 765	Facts: Pickin argued that the correct procedure had not been followed when passing an Act of Parliament. Lord Reid: *'The idea that a court is entitled to disregard a provision in an Act of Parliament on any ground must seem strange and startling to anyone with any knowledge of the history and law of our constitution.'*

See also Lord Reid's statement in the *Madzimbamuto* case (Section 6.4.1, above).

6.4.3 Parliament cannot bind itself

Parliament cannot enact legislation that cannot be altered or repealed by Parliament at some future date.

Parliament can repeal or amend legislation either expressly or impliedly.

> **Definition**
>
> **Express repeal:** Explicit words in an Act of Parliament revoking all or part of an earlier Act.
> **Implied repeal:** Where a later Act of Parliament conflicts with an earlier one, the courts take the later to have amended the earlier as much as is necessary to resolve the conflict.

Cases:	
Vauxhall Estates v Liverpool Corporation [1932] 1 KB 733	Facts: A 1925 Act of Parliament conflicted with a 1919 Act. Vauxhall Estates argued that the 1919 Act was worded in such a way that it could not be overridden by the later Act. Held: Parliament cannot enact legislation that cannot be altered by a future Act of Parliament.
Ellen St Estates v Minister of Health [1934] KB 590	Facts: The facts here are similar to the *Vauxhall* case. Ellen St Estates argued that while Parliament could expressly repeal the 1919 Act, it could not impliedly repeal it. Held: All Acts of Parliament can be amended expressly or impliedly.

Because legislation can be amended or repealed expressly or impliedly, it is not possible for Parliament to entrench legislation, i.e. to protect it from future amendment.

Workpoint

Read the following quotation. Explain in your own words Dicey's argument as to why Parliament cannot entrench legislation.

'The logical reason why Parliament has failed in its endeavours to enact unchallengeable enactments is that a sovereign power cannot, while retaining its sovereign character, restrict its own powers by any parliamentary enactment.'

(Dicey, A.V., *Introduction to the Study of the Law of the Constitution*, 10th edn, 1959, London: Macmillan [1898])

6.4.4 Parliament can legislate for any time or any place

6.4.4.1 Time

Most legislation has prospective effect: it alters the legal position from the date it takes legal effect. However, Parliament is able to enact legislation that has retrospective effect: it alters the legal position retrospectively.

Cases:	
Burmah Oil v Lord Advocate [1965] AC 75	The House of Lords held that damage done to Burmah Oil's property during the Second World War was lawful but the Government should compensate Burmah Oil for its losses.
	Parliament enacted the War Damage Act 1965 which stated that no person shall be entitled to compensation for damage done during, or in preparation for, war. The Act had retrospective effect, which nullified the decision awarding compensation to Burmah Oil.
R v Londonderry Justices, ex parte Hume [1972] NI 91	The Court of Appeal in Northern Ireland held that the arrest and detention of suspects by the army was unlawful.
	Parliament enacted the Northern Ireland Act 1972 which stated that the army had the necessary powers of arrest at the relevant time (i.e. it had retrospective effect).

6.4.4.2 Place

Parliament can legislate for any geographical area; its legislative competence is not confined by the UK boundary.

This has famously been captured by Sir Ivor Jennings:

'Parliamentary supremacy means that Parliament can legislate for all persons and all places. If it enacts that smoking in the streets of Paris is an offence, then it is an offence.'

(Jennings, I., *The Law and the Constitution*, 5th edn, 1959, London: Hodder & Stoughton)

There are a number of statutes in which Parliament has legislated for areas outside the UK.

- The Continental Shelf Act 1964 vests rights of exploration and exploitation of the continental shelf (the waters surrounding the UK) in the Crown and extends criminal and civil liability to installations placed on the waters above the continental shelf.

- The War Crimes Act 1991 provides for criminal proceedings for certain crimes committed in territories controlled by Germany during the Second World War.

- The Sexual Offences Act 2003 allows for prosecution for acts done in countries or territories outside of the UK.

Checkpoint – The traditional view of parliamentary supremacy

Item on checklist:	Done!
I can explain the traditional view of parliamentary supremacy in one or two sentences.	
I know the four interrelated rules that make up the traditional view of parliamentary supremacy and I can provide case law authority for each of them.	

6.5 Possible qualifications of parliamentary supremacy

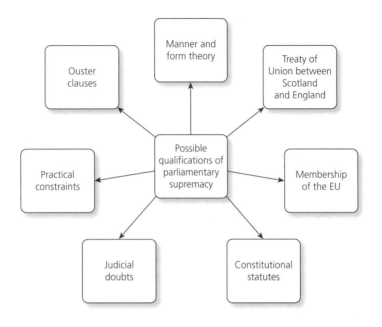

6.5.1 Manner and form theory

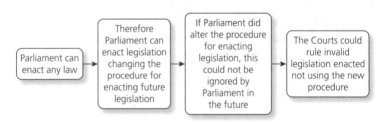

Manner and form theorists argue that Parliament can legislate to alter the procedure by which Acts of Parliament are enacted or, to say virtually the same thing, Parliament can alter the criteria by which courts will recognise an Act of Parliament to be valid.

This contrasts with Lord Campbell's statement in the *Edinburgh and Dalkeith Railway* case (Section 6.4.2, above) that, as long as an Act of Parliament has been passed by the Commons, Lords and received royal assent, the courts will not look for anything else or in detail at the procedure followed when enacting legislation.

An example might prove useful in understanding manner and form (you might want to read this more than once).

> Imagine that Parliament enacts the (fictitious) Protection of Rights Act 2011 which states that any attempt to amend or repeal the Human Rights Act 1998 must be supported by a two-thirds majority in the both the House of Commons and the House of Lords.
>
> This would be an attempt to alter the way in which some types of legislation could be enacted in future: instead of a simple majority in each House (i.e. 50 per cent + 1), legislation amending the Human Rights Act 1998 must be enacted by a two-thirds majority.
>
> Now, imagine that in 2012 Parliament enacts the (fictitious) British Rights Act 2012 which amends the Human Rights Act 1998 but is passed by the normal simple majority in the Commons and the Lords rather than the special majority required by the (fictitious) Protection of Rights Act 2011.

Question: If someone attempted to challenge the validity of the (fictitious) British Rights Act 2012 in the courts on the grounds that it had not been enacted following the procedure specified in the (fictitious) Protection of Rights Act 2011, what would the courts do?

- Would they rule that if an Act of Parliament has been passed by the Commons, Lords and received royal assent (as per Lord Campbell in the *Edinburgh and Dalkeith Railway* case) it is valid and they will not look any deeper than that at, say, the majority which enacted the legislation under challenge?

or

- Would they rule, as the manner and form theorists claim, that Parliament can alter any law, including the law governing the procedure by which legislation is enacted? Thus, if Parliament has not followed the procedure established by the (fictitious) Protection of Rights Act 2011 then the courts may rule the legislation invalid.

> Note: Nobody knows the answer to this question until it arises and the courts rule on it. However, as we will see below, there has been some relevant case law from other jurisdictions and some *obiter dicta* in the *Jackson* case.

Contrasting views	
The traditional view	**Manner and form**
If Parliament can alter the criteria by which the courts decide whether an Act of Parliament is valid then it will effectively be able to bind itself – it could, for instance, require future legislation to be enacted by a procedure that is practically unachievable. For instance, Parliament might enact that, in future, legislation on a particular matter must be passed by the Commons, Lords, receive royal assent *and* be supported by a referendum in which 90% of the population vote in favour of the legislation.	If Parliament can make any law then it can alter the criteria by which the courts decide whether an Act of Parliament is valid.

6.5.1.1 Manner and form: a possible example

Human Rights Act 1998, s 19:

1) A Minister of the Crown in charge of a Bill in either House of Parliament must, before Second Reading of the Bill –
   a) make a statement to the effect that in his view the provisions of the Bill are compatible with the Convention rights (*'a statement of compatibility'*); or
   b) make a statement to the effect that although he is unable to make a statement of compatibility the government nevertheless wishes the House to proceed with the Bill.

2) The statement must be in writing and be published in such manner as the Minister making it considers appropriate.

Section 19 of the Human Rights Act 1998 seems to introduce an extra procedural step when enacting legislation: that the minister in charge of getting the Bill through either House of Parliament must make a written statement as to whether or not the proposed legislation is compatible with the rights guaranteed by the European Convention on Human Rights.

The question, again, is what would the courts do if legislation was enacted without such a statement? Would they rule the legislation to be invalid because it had not been enacted following the procedure established by the Human Rights Act or would they follow the traditional approach and rule that as long as the legislation has been passed by the Commons, Lords and received royal assent it is valid legislation?

6.5.1.2 Manner and form: some cases

Cases:	
Attorney-General of New South Wales v Trethowan [1932] AC 526	Facts: Legislation abolishing the upper House of the New South Wales legislature was not supported by a referendum as required by earlier legislation. Held: The legislation attempting to abolish the upper House was not valid because the correct procedure had not been followed.
Harris v Minister of the Interior [1952] (2) SA 428	Facts: Legislation depriving black South Africans of the right to vote was not enacted as required by the South African Constitution. Held: The legislation had not been enacted in the correct manner and was therefore invalid.
Bribery Commissioner v Ranasinghe [1965] AC 172	Facts: Legislation creating a new judicial office, effectively altering the Ceylon Constitution, was not certified by the Speaker as having been passed by a two-thirds majority as required by the constitution. Held: Without the certification of the Speaker, the legislation was not valid.

The above three cases are from jurisdictions without a supreme legislature so the degree to which they can be relied on in the UK situation is questionable. However, two Law Lords in the following case made *obiter* statements supporting manner and form theory.

Case:	
R (Jackson) v Attorney-General [2006] 1 AC 262	Facts: The Hunting Act 2004 had been passed using the procedure in the Parliament Acts 1911 and 1949. Jackson argued that the 1949 Act and, consequently, the 2004 Act were not valid.
	Held: The 1949 Act was valid, which meant that legislation enacted under it, including the Hunting Act 2004, was also valid.
	Lord Steyn: *'But, apart from the traditional method of law making, Parliament ... may functionally redistribute legislative power in different ways. For example, Parliament could for specific purposes provide for a two-thirds majority in the House of Commons and the House of Lords. This would involve a redefinition of Parliament for a specific purpose. Such redefinition could not be disregarded.'*
	Baroness Hale: *'[I]f Parliament is required to pass legislation on particular matters in a particular way, then Parliament is not permitted to ignore those requirements when passing legislation on those matters, nor is it permitted to remove or relax those requirements by passing legislation in the ordinary way.'*

Workpoint

In the *Jackson* case, Baroness Hale relied on the Parliament Acts 1911 and 1949 as support for manner and form:

'If the sovereign Parliament can redefine itself downwards, to remove or modify the requirement for the consent of the Upper House, it may very well be that it can also redefine itself upwards, to require a particular parliamentary majority or a popular referendum for particular types of measure. In each case, the courts would be respecting the will of the sovereign Parliament as constituted when that will had been expressed.'

Explain her argument.

6.5.2 Treaty of Union between Scotland and England

Prior to 1707, Scotland and England were separate countries, each with their own parliaments: the English Parliament and the Scottish Parliament (not to be confused with the Scottish Parliament that exists today, which was established by the Scotland Act 1998).

In 1706 Scotland and England negotiated the Treaty of Union by which they agreed to unite to form the United Kingdom of Great Britain. As part of this agreement, the English and Scottish Parliaments agreed to unite to form the UK Parliament.

The Treaty of Union took effect on 1 May 1707.

> Note: Following the agreement to form the United Kingdom, the Scottish Parliament enacted the Union with England Act and the English Parliament enacted the Union with Scotland Act. These are collectively known as the Acts of Union and they reproduced the terms of the Treaty of Union.

The relevance for parliamentary supremacy
The Treaty of Union seems to guarantee the continued existence of certain things:

- Article 1 states that the union between England and Scotland is to last forever (i.e. it cannot be broken).

- Article 18 prevents Scottish private law from being altered unless it is for the obvious benefit of the Scottish people.

- Article 19 states that the Court of Session in Scotland should continue in existence for all time with the same rights and privileges as it had before the Union.

The argument is that, because the Treaty of Union is the document that established the UK Parliament, the guarantees given in the Treaty cannot be breached by Parliament. If true, these matters are beyond the legislative competence of Parliament and it cannot be said that Parliament can enact any law.

Workpoint

Imagine the UK Parliament enacted legislation attempting to break the Union so that Scotland became a separate country, and that the validity of this legislation was challenged in the courts. What arguments could be marshalled in favour or against its validity?

Cases:	
MacCormick v Lord Advocate (1953) SC 396	Lord Cooper: *'The principle of unlimited sovereignty of Parliament is a distinctly English principle which has no counterpart in Scottish Constitutional Law ... Considering that the Union legislation extinguished the Parliaments of Scotland and England and replaced them by a new Parliament, I have difficulty in seeing why the new Parliament of Great Britain must inherit all the peculiar characteristics of the English Parliament but none of the Scottish Parliament as if all that happened in 1707 was that Scottish representatives were admitted to the Parliament of England. That is not what was done. Further, the Treaty and the associated legislation, by which the Parliament of Great Britain was brought into existence as the successor of the separate Parliaments of Scotland and England, contain some clauses which expressly reserve to the Parliament of Great Britain powers of subsequent modification, and other clauses which contain no such power or emphatically exclude subsequent alteration by declarations that the provision shall be fundamental and unalterable in all time coming, or declarations of a like effect. I have never been able to understand how it is possible to reconcile with elementary canons of construction the adoption by the English constitutional theorists of the same attitude to these remarkably different types of provisions ... I have not found in the Union legislation any provision that the Parliament of Great Britain should be "absolutely sovereign" in the sense that Parliament should be free to alter the Treaty at will.'*

Gibson v Lord Advocate [1975] 1 CMLR 563	Lord Keith declined to rule on whether a legislative provision was for the benefit of the Scottish people, though he indicated that he might be prepared to rule on the validity of other types of legislation:
	'I prefer to preserve my opinion on what the position would be if the United Kingdom Parliament passed an Act purporting to abolish the Court of Session of the Church of Scotland or to substitute English Law for the whole body of Scots Law.'

Workpoint

Analyse Lord Cooper's argument in the *MacCormick* case. What is his point when he says that parliamentary sovereignty is an English not a Scottish phenomenon? Why does he think it is not possible to reconcile the *'elementary canons of construction'* with the view of English constitutional theorists about parliamentary supremacy?

6.5.2.1 Union with Ireland

At the beginning of the 1800s there was an agreement between Britain and Ireland to form the United Kingdom of Great Britain and Ireland. This agreement was ratified by the British and Irish Parliaments, each passing an Act of Union.

Like the Treaty of Union between Scotland and England, the Acts of Union also guaranteed that the union was to last forever; it also stated that the Church in Ireland was to remain the established (i.e. official) church forever.

Neither of these guarantees has lasted.

• The Irish Church Act 1869 disestablished the Church in Ireland.

Case:	
Ex parte Canon Selwyn (1872) 36 JP 54	Facts: Canon Selwyn attempted to challenge the validity of the Irish Church Act 1869 on the ground that it contravened the Acts of Union. Held: This was not a justiciable matter.

- The Republic of Ireland is no longer part of the United Kingdom: the Irish Free State (Agreement) Act 1922 gave southern Ireland a self-governing status within the British Empire and the Ireland Act 1949 recognised the Republic of Ireland as a sovereign independent state.

The fact that the guarantees in the British/Irish Acts of Union have not lasted may bring into question the similar guarantees in the Treaty of Union between Scotland and England.

There are two possible views.

a) The breach of the guarantees in the Acts of Union between Britain and Ireland demonstrates that such guarantees are not binding on Parliament.

b) The Treaty of Union between Scotland and England is more fundamental and of greater importance than the Acts of Union between Britain and Ireland. Thus, the breach of guarantees in the latter does not necessarily mean that the guarantees in the former are not binding.

6.5.3 Parliamentary supremacy and membership of the European Union

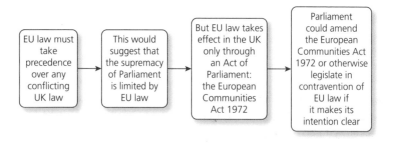

The UK joined the European Economic Community (now the EU) on 1 January 1973. It is a principle of EU law that it takes precedence over any conflicting law of the member states. This has implications for parliamentary supremacy because it seems to imply that Parliament cannot legislate in a way that conflicts with EU law. At first sight, this seems to be the inference we can take from the following case.

Case:	
R v Secretary of State for Transport, ex parte Factortame Ltd and Others (No. 2) [1991] AC 603	Facts: Factortame challenged the Merchant Shipping Act 1988 on the ground that it breached EC law. They sought an interim injunction to prevent the relevant provisions of the Act taking effect while the case was decided. Among other things, it was argued that the Crown Proceedings Act 1947 prevented such injunctions being given.
	Held: After seeking advice from the European Court of Justice, the House of Lords granted the injunction.

The *Factortame* case appears to infringe the traditional view of parliamentary supremacy in two ways.

a) We saw above (Section 6.4.2) that the traditional view is that the courts cannot question an Act of Parliament or rule it to be invalid. Given this, they certainly should not be able to grant an injunction preventing an Act taking effect.

b) The Crown Proceedings Act 1947 prevented such injunctions being granted but the European Court of Justice stated that this rule should be set aside, which the House of Lords duly did.

It would be easy to conclude from the *Factortame* case that parliamentary supremacy had been limited by membership of the EU.

However, we must remember that EU law only takes effect in the UK by virtue of an Act of Parliament – the European Communities Act 1972 – and Parliament could amend or repeal that Act to alter the influence of EU law on UK law. This seemed to be acknowledged in the following case.

Case:	
Macarthys v Smith [1979] ICR 785	Lord Denning: *'I ... make one observation on a constitutional point. Thus far I have assumed that our Parliament, whenever it passes legislation, intends to fulfil its obligations under the [EC] Treaty. If the time should come when our Parliament deliberately passes an Act – with the intention of repudiating the Treaty or any provision in it – and says*

so in express terms – then I should have thought that it would be the duty of the courts to follow the statute of our Parliament.'

Lawton LJ: *'Parliament's recognition of European Community law and of the jurisdiction of the European Court of Justice by one enactment can be withdrawn by another.'*

6.5.4 Constitutional statutes

Case:	
Thoburn v Sunderland City Council [2003] QB 151	Laws LJ: *'There are now classes or types of legislative provision which cannot be repealed by mere implication.* . . . *We should recognise a hierarchy of Acts of Parliament: as it were "ordinary" statutes and "constitutional" statutes.'*

Laws LJ's suggestion that there is a hierarchy of statutes and that the implied repeal rule (above, Section 6.4.3) does not apply to constitutional statutes is *obiter* only. Yet, it is a statement made by a senior judge and should therefore be taken seriously. Its importance is that it departs from the traditional view of parliamentary supremacy in two ways.

a) It conflicts with the view that all Acts of Parliament are of equivalent legal status.

b) It conflicts with the view that any Act of Parliament can be amended as easily as another.

We can see this conflict when we contrast Laws LJ's statement with Dicey's view:

'Parliamentary sovereignty [means]: first, the power of the legislature to alter any law, fundamental or otherwise, as freely and in the same manner as other laws; secondly, the absence of any legal distinction between constitutional and other laws.'

(Dicey, A.V., *Introduction to the Study of the Law of the Constitution* 10th edn, 1959, London: Macmillan [1898])

6.5.5 Judicial doubts about parliamentary supremacy

A number of senior judges have expressed doubts about whether Parliament's legislative powers are unlimited. These doubts have been given both extra-judicially (e.g. in academic articles, lectures or interviews) and when judging.

Case:	
R (Jackson) v Attorney-General [2006] 1 AC 262	See Section 6.5.1.2, above. Lord Steyn: *'The classic account given by Dicey of the doctrine of the supremacy of Parliament, pure and absolute as it was, can now be seen to be out of place in the modern United Kingdom.... In exceptional circumstances involving an attempt to abolish judicial review or the ordinary role of the courts, the ... Supreme Court may have to consider whether this is a constitutional fundamental which even a sovereign Parliament ... cannot abolish.'* Lord Hope: *'[P]arliamentary sovereignty is no longer, if it ever was, absolute. It is not uncontrolled ... It is no longer right to say that its freedom to legislate admits of no qualification whatever.'* Baroness Hale: *'The courts will treat with particular suspicion (and might even reject) any attempt to subvert the rule of law by removing governmental action affecting the rights of the individual from all judicial scrutiny.'*

Lord Woolf has written:

'I myself would consider there were advantages in making it clear that ultimately there are even limits on the supremacy of Parliament which it is the courts' inalienable responsibility to identify and uphold.'
(Lord Woolf of Barnes, *'Droit Public* – English Style' [1995] *Public Law* 57)

However, you should note that these views are not shared by all judges, and may not even represent the views of the majority of judges. See, for instance, Lord Bingham's comments in the *Jackson* case (again).

Case:	
R (Jackson) v Attorney-General [2006] 1 AC 262	Lord Bingham: *'The bedrock of the British constitution is . . . the supremacy of the Crown in Parliament. . . . Then, as now, the Crown in Parliament was unconstrained by any entrenched or codified constitution. It could make or unmake any law it wished.'*

In a lecture in 2011, Lord Neuberger, the then Master of the Rolls, expressed support for the traditional, absolute view of parliamentary supremacy and questioned the contrary position taken by Baroness Hale and Lords Steyn and Hope in the *Jackson* case (Lord Neuberger of Abbotsbury, 'Who Are the Masters Now?', Second Lord Alexander of Weedon Lecture, 6 April 2011).

6.5.6 Practical constraints on legislative supremacy

It is all very well saying that Parliament could ban smoking on the streets of Paris (above, Section 6.4.4.2) but this is unlikely to happen and would have little effect on the lives of Parisians if it did. Similar views about the distinction between what may be possible in legal theory and what is possible in reality have been expressed by some judges.

Cases:	
British Coal Corporation v The King [1935] AC 500	Viscount Sankey LC: *'It is doubtless true that the power of . . . Parliament to pass on its own initiative any legislation that it thought fit extending to Canada remains in theory unimpaired . . . But that is theory and has no relation to realities.'*
Blackburn v Attorney-General [1971] 1 WLR 1037	Lord Denning MR: *'Take the Statute of Westminster 1931, which takes away the power of Parliament to legislate for the Dominions. Can anyone imagine that Parliament could or would reverse that statute? Take the Acts that have granted independence to the Dominions and territories overseas. Can anyone imagine that Parliament could or would reverse these laws and take away their independence? Most clearly not. Freedom once given cannot be taken away.'*

6.5.7 Ouster clauses

An ouster clause is a provision in an Act of Parliament that seems to restrict or exclude the courts' jurisdiction over a particular matter. Under the traditional view of parliamentary supremacy, the courts should give effect to such clauses. However, the courts have often decided that such clauses do not oust their jurisdiction. The most famous case concerning an ouster clause is the *Anisminic* case.

Case:	
***Anisminic Ltd v Foreign Compensation Commission* [1969] 2 AC 147**	Facts: Anisminic wanted to challenge a decision made by the Foreign Compensation Commission. However, s 4(4) of the Foreign Compensation Act 1950 read: *'The determination by the Commission of any application ... shall not be called in question in any court of law.'*
	Held: The majority of the House of Lords held that s 4(4) did not prevent them reviewing the legality of the decision in question.

The courts' treatment of ouster clauses is often explained as mere interpretation of them. However, it is difficult to see this approach as interpretation when it appears to result in the exact opposite of their plain meaning and leaves such clauses without any effect.

Wade and Forsyth write that the policy of the courts with respect to ouster clauses '*thus becomes one of total disobedience to Parliament*' (Wade, H.W.R. and Forsyth, C.F., *Administrative Law*, 10th edn, 2009, Oxford: Oxford University Press).

Checklist – Possible qualifications of the traditional view of parliamentary supremacy.	
Item on checklist:	**Done!**
I can explain the way in which the following may limit parliamentary supremacy and evaluate the degree to which they do, in fact, qualify the traditional view: • manner and form theory • constitutional statutes • Treaty of Union between • judicial doubts Scotland and England • practical constraints • membership of the EU • ouster clauses.	

Research Point

Find out how many times the Parliament Acts have been used to enact legislation and name the Acts in question.

Research Point

Read the *Jackson* case [2006] 1 AC 262. Explain Jackson's argument that the Parliament Act 1949 and, consequently, the Hunting Act 2004 was not valid.

Research Point

Read the *Factortame* case [1991] AC 603. Write a concise account of the facts and decision.

Potential exam question

Explain the ways in which parliamentary sovereignty may be limited in the UK.

Chapter 7
Monarchy and the royal prerogative

In this chapter, you will learn about:

- the rules governing the succession to the throne;

- the role of the monarch as Head of State and in the three arms of state;

- the royal prerogative.

7.1 The monarch

We saw in Section 2.5 that the UK's constitution is classified as monarchical, rather than republican, according to K.C. Wheare's suggested classifications. This is because the Head of State is a monarch.

The monarch's position in the UK is unique and is one where initial appearance conflicts with reality:

- She seems to be the pivotal figure of much of the constitutional and political machinery of the UK but, in fact, her role is largely symbolic.

- She seems to possess enormous power yet, in reality, she exercises very little (if any) personal political power.

- She is the only constitutional actor who is a member of all three arms of state: the executive, the legislature and the judiciary (see Section 5.3.1); however, as we shall see, her role in each arm of state is mostly – and in some cases wholly – ceremonial or formal.

The contradiction between the monarch's apparent power and the reality is epitomised to some degree by the State Opening of Parliament in which she formally opens Parliament for the new parliamentary session, making a speech to the Lords and the Commons outlining the Government's proposed legislation. Here, she plays the central role but her actions are wholly dictated by tradition and the speech she reads is written for her by ministers.

This situation, whereby the monarch's powers are limited so that she exercises no real political power, is sometimes referred to as a constitutional or limited monarchy and is distinguished in this regard from strong or absolute monarchies.

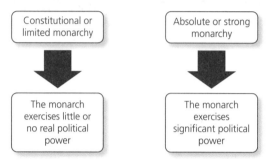

7.1.1 Some basic terms

One possible area of confusion for students is the different terms that are sometimes used to refer to the monarch. Terms such as the Queen, the Sovereign, the Crown and the monarch are often used interchangeably – and, indeed, are often synonymous – but can mean different things in different contexts. Simply speaking, these terms have the following meaning.

> **Definition**
>
> **The Crown:** In the UK, this can refer to the monarch or the institution of monarchy. It may also refer to the Government.
>
> **Monarch:** A King or Queen who is the ruler of a state and holds the position of head of the monarchy.
>
> **Queen:** The title of the sovereign, if she is female, or the title of the wife of a male sovereign (the King).
>
> **Sovereign:** The ruler of a state: the person who holds the position of King or Queen.

7.2 Succession

Succession to the throne of the United Kingdom happens automatically: the next in line to the throne becomes monarch at the instant of death of the previous monarch without the need for any ceremony or coronation.

Succession to the throne is governed by a number of principles.

- Succession is dictated by the hereditary principle whereby the heirs of the existing monarch are her successors to the throne.

- Currently, precedence is given to the eldest male heirs and their children. This is so even if there is an older female heir.
  - For example, Queen Victoria's eldest child, Princess Victoria, was female yet priority for succession to the throne was given to her younger brothers and their children over her.

- The Act of Settlement 1700 prohibits Roman Catholics, or those married to a Roman Catholic, from succeeding to the throne.

> <u>Note</u>: At the time of writing, the Government is trying to pilot the Succession to the Crown Bill through Parliament. This makes changes the rules of succession in two ways:
> - The eldest child of Prince William will succeed to the throne regardless of gender.
> - Those marrying a Catholic will not be prohibited from becoming or remaining monarch.

Workpoint

List the advantages and disadvantages of having a hereditary monarchy as a system of government.

7.3 The role of the monarch

The monarch has a number of roles within the UK constitution.

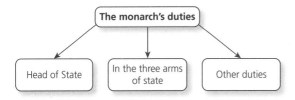

7.3.1 Head of State

The monarch is the Head of State in the UK. The Head of State is the person who acts as the official public representative of a state on the national and international stage. The Head of State is also the supreme executive officer of a state even if, as in the UK, this position is largely nominal.

The Queen is also the Head of State of 15 other countries: Antigua and Barbuda, Australia, the Bahamas, Barbados, Belize, Canada, Grenada, Jamaica, New Zealand, Papua New Guinea, the Solomon Islands, St Christopher and Nevis, St Lucia, St Vincent and the Grenadines, and Tuvalu.

7.3.2 The monarch's role in the three arms of state

As noted above, the monarch has a role in each of the three arms of state: the executive, the legislature and the judiciary.

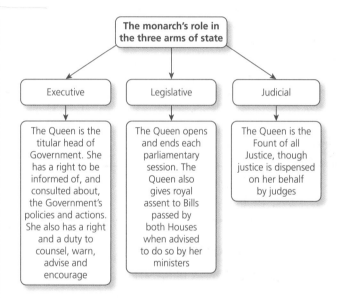

7.3.2.1 The monarch's role in the executive

Nominally, the Queen is the head of the Government – it is, after all, Her Majesty's Government. However, the de facto head of Government is the Prime Minister and the Queen's executive powers are exercised on her behalf by her ministers. Thus, her role is largely symbolic.

However, that is not to say that the Queen has no real part to play. Writing in the nineteenth century, Walter Bagehot wrote:

'[T]he sovereign has, under a constitutional monarchy such as ours, three rights – the right to be consulted, the right to encourage, the right to warn.'

(Bagehot, W., *The English Constitution*, 1867, London: Chapman and Hall, p. 103)

Similarly, on 29 July 1986, the Queen's Private Secretary, Sir William Heseltine, wrote to *The Times* newspaper stating the following with regard to her relationship with Government:

• The Queen has the right and duty to counsel, warn and encourage her Government and, consequently, is entitled to have and express opinions to the Prime Minister.

• The Queen is obliged to act on the advice of her ministers.

• Communications between the Queen and Prime Minister must remain confidential.

In order to exercise the right and duty to be consulted, to warn, to counsel and to encourage the Queen must be informed of Government policies and decisions. This happens in two main ways:

• She receives all Cabinet papers and the minutes of Cabinet meetings as well as other significant Government papers.

• She has a weekly audience with the Prime Minister at which the Prime Minister informs the Queen of the Government's plans and actions and she is able to express her opinion.

7.3.2.2 The monarch's role in the legislature

The monarch is one of three bodies that compose Parliament, along with the House of Commons and the House of Lords (see Section 6.1). She opens, and brings to an end, each session of Parliament.

Definition

Parliamentary session: The parliamentary year, beginning with the State Opening of Parliament.

The Queen also gives royal assent to Bills that have been passed by both Houses. However, as noted in Chapter 3, the conventional rule is that the monarch gives royal assent to all Bills when advised to do so by her ministers (see Section 3.2).

7.3.2.3 *The monarch's role in the judiciary*

Formally speaking, the monarch is the Fount (source) of Justice in the UK. However, her power to dispense justice has been irrevocably delegated to judges and she cannot personally participate in legal proceedings.

Case:	
Prohibitions del Roy (1607) 12 Co Rep 63	Facts: King James I claimed the right to determine a legal dispute.
	Held: The right of the King to personally administer justice no longer existed and he cannot order anyone to be arrested.
	Coke CJ: *'[T]he King in his own person cannot adjudge any case, either criminal, as treason, felony, etc or betwixt party and party, concerning his inheritance, chattels, or goods, etc but this ought to be determined and adjudged in some Court of Justice, according to the law and custom of England.'*

7.3.3 Other duties

The Queen also has many other roles, including:

• She is the Commander in Chief of the Armed Forces.

• She is the Head of the Church of England and Defender of the Faith.

• She is the Head of the Commonwealth.

> **Definition**
>
> **The Commonwealth:** A voluntary organisation of 54 nations, developed out of the British Empire. All but two nations, Rwanda and Mozambique, were part of the British Empire. The Head of the Commonwealth is the Queen.

• She gives formal consent to the appointment of, among others: ministers, Bishops of the Church of England, senior judges.

• Formally, she appoints the First Ministers of Scotland and Wales.

- She represents the UK internationally and receives foreign diplomatic representatives.

- She confers all titles of honour (knighthoods, damehoods, OBEs, etc.).

- She is responsible for the good government of the self-governing Crown Dependencies: the Channel Islands and the Isle of Man.

Checkpoint – The monarch	
Item on checklist:	**Done!**
I can explain what is meant by the term 'constitutional monarchy'.	
I can explain the principles governing succession to the throne in the UK.	
I can briefly explain the monarch's role as Head of State.	
I can give an account of the monarch's role in the three arms of state.	
I can give an account of the monarch's other roles.	

7.4 The royal prerogative

Historically, the royal prerogative refers to the common law powers of the monarch to govern, including powers to legislate and administer justice. However, over the centuries it became less and less appropriate for such powers to be exercised directly by a hereditary monarch. Nowadays, most prerogative powers are exercised on the monarch's behalf by her ministers (or judges in the case of the power to administer justice) or, where they are exercised by the monarch, their exercise is governed by constitutional convention.

There are, though, some aspects of the prerogative that represent a personal choice by the Queen – for instance, while most honours are bestowed by the monarch on the advice of the Prime Minister or other ministers, there are some that are in the personal gift of the Queen. These are: Medals for Long Service; the Order of Merit; the Order of the Garter; the Order of the Thistle; Royal Medals of Honour; the Royal Victorian Chain; and the Royal Victorian Order.

7.4.1 Definition and characteristics

Writing in the eighteenth century, William Blackstone defined the royal prerogative in the following way:

'By the word prerogative we usually understand that special pre-eminence, which the king hath, over and above all other persons, and out of the ordinary course of the common law, in right of his regal dignity. It signifies ... something that is required or demanded before, or in preference to, all others. And hence it follows, that it must be in its nature singular and eccentrical; that it can only be applied to those rights and capacities which the king enjoys alone, in contradistinction to others, and not to those which he enjoys in common with any of his subjects.'

(Blackstone, W., *Commentaries on the Laws of England*, 1765–1769, Oxford: Clarendon Press)

Dicey describes the royal prerogative as:

'The residue of discretionary or arbitrary authority, which at any given time is legally left in the hands of the Crown.'

(Dicey, A.V., *Introduction to the Study of the Law of the Constitution*, 10th edn, 1959, London: Macmillan [1898], p. 424)

From these definitions we can ascribe the following characteristics to the royal prerogative:

- The powers exercised by virtue of the prerogative are unique to the Crown.

- It is derived from the common law – this means that the courts are the final arbiter of whether a particular prerogative power exists.

- It is residual in the sense that it is the remaining power of the monarch.

7.4.2 The extent of the prerogative

There is no definitive list of all the prerogative powers that exist. Bradley and Ewing have listed the main areas where the prerogative is currently exercised (Bradley, A.W. and Ewing, K.D., *Constitutional and Administrative Law*, 15th edn, 2011, London: Longman).

- *'Powers relating to the legislature'* including: the power to summon, prorogue and dissolve Parliament (subject to the terms of the Fixed-Term Parliaments Act 2011 (see Section 4.3.1.3)); give royal assent to Bills; and legislate by Orders in Council or letters patent.

- *'Powers relating to the judicial system'* including: certain functions undertaken by the Attorney General and (in Scotland) the Lord Advocate; the power to pardon convicted offenders; and the power to grant leave to appeal to the Judicial Committee of the Privy Council.

- *'Powers relating to foreign affairs'* including: the power to make treaties; the making of war or declaration of peace; the power to issue passports.

- *'Powers relating to the armed forces'*: the monarch is the Commander in Chief of the Armed Forces and their organisation and deployment operates under the prerogative.

- *'Appointments and honours'* including: the appointment of ministers, judges and other holders of public office; the conferment of honours and decorations; and the creation of peers.

- *'Immunities and privileges'* including: the personal immunity of the sovereign from being sued; and the courts assume that statutes do not bind the Crown unless they expressly state otherwise.

- *'The prerogative in times of emergency'*: the prerogative may allow things in times of emergency for the conduct of war or to defend the Realm, such as the requisitioning of ships (with compensation).

- *'Miscellaneous prerogatives'* including: the right to create corporations by royal charter; and the right to mine precious metals.

Workpoint

From your existing knowledge, try to identify some of the above powers that are:

a) exercised by the monarch, though their exercise is governed by constitutional convention;
b) exercised in reality by ministers and others.

7.4.3 The prerogative and the courts

The courts have the power to recognise the existence and extent of existing prerogative powers. However, there is no power to create new prerogative powers.

Cases:	
The Case of Proclamations [1611] 12 Co Rep 74	Coke CJ: *'The King hath no prerogative but that which the law of the land allows him.'*
BBC v Johns [1965] Ch 32	Diplock LJ: *'It is 350 years and a civil war too late for the Queen's courts to broaden the prerogative. The limits within which the executive government may impose obligations or restraints on citizens of the United Kingdom without any statutory authority are now well settled and incapable of extension.'*

The courts also have the power to review the exercise of prerogative power, as long as it is justiciable (i.e. suitable for judicial determination).

Cases:	
R v Criminal Injuries Compensation Board, ex parte Lain [1967] 2 QB 864	Facts: It was argued that because a Criminal Compensation Board was established by the royal prerogative rather than by statute it was not amenable to judicial control. Held: The Board was amenable to judicial review.
Council of Civil Service Unions v Minister for the Civil Service [1985] AC 374	Facts: An Order in Council was issued under the prerogative prohibiting employees at GCHQ from belonging to a trade union. This was challenged by the unions and it was argued by counsel for the Government that, because the Order was enacted under the prerogative, it was immune from review. Held: An Order in Council was not immune from judicial review simply because it was enacted under the prerogative. However, Lord Roskill did state that, because of their nature, some powers would be non-justiciable: *'Prerogative powers such as those relating to the making of treaties, the defence of the realm, the prerogative of mercy, the grant of honours, the dissolution of Parliament and the appointment of ministers as well as others are not, I think, susceptible to judicial review because their nature and subject matter are such as not to be amenable to the judicial process.'*

7.4.4 The prerogative and statute

Because of parliamentary sovereignty, Parliament may, by an Act of Parliament, restrict, extinguish or preserve a prerogative power. Further, where a statute regulates a matter that previously operated under the prerogative, the statute will prevail while it exists. This can be seen in the following two cases.

Cases:	
***Attorney General v de Keyser's Royal Hotel Ltd* [1920] AC 508**	Facts: The Government took over the hotel for wartime purposes. The question was whether compensation was payable under the prerogative or under the more generous Defence of the Realm Act 1914. Held: The prerogative was in abeyance for the life of the statute.
***R v Secretary of State for the Home Department, ex parte Fire Brigades Union* [1995] 2 AC 513**	Facts: The Criminal Justice Act 1988 established a criminal injuries compensation scheme and gave the Home Secretary the power to decide when to bring the scheme into effect. The Government announced that it would not bring the statutory scheme into effect but would replace it with a less generous scheme to be created under the royal prerogative. Held: The Home Secretary was under a continuous duty to consider when to bring the statutory scheme into effect and could not exercise the prerogative in a way that conflicted with that duty.

Checkpoint – The royal prerogative

Item on checklist:	Done!
I can give an account of the characteristics of the royal prerogative.	
I can give some examples of the exercise of prerogative power and distinguish among those that are exercised by the monarch on the advice of ministers, those that are exercised by ministers and those that are exercised at the monarch's personal discretion.	

Checkpoint – The royal prerogative

Item on checklist:	Done!
I can explain the powers that the courts have with regard to prerogative powers.	
I can explain the relationship between the prerogative and Acts of Parliament.	

Potential exam question

Explain why the UK is considered to be a constitutional, rather than a strong or absolute, monarchy.

Chapter 8
The rule of law

In this chapter, you will learn:

- the basic meaning of the rule of law;

- the meaning of government according to law;

- different versions of the rule of law by Dicey, Raz and Lord Bingham;

- the difference between procedural and substantive versions of the rule of law;

- the potential conflict between parliamentary supremacy and the rule of law.

8.1 Introduction

Constitutional Reform Act 2005, s 1:

This Act does not adversely affect–

a) *the existing constitutional principle of the rule of law, or*
b) *the Lord Chancellor's existing constitutional role in relation to that principle.*

The Constitutional Reform Act 2005 may state it does not adversely affect the principle of the rule of law, but there is no guidance in the legislation about what the principle is or what it requires. In one sense, this is not surprising because, as we will see, there are many different versions of the rule of law.

The rule of law is a topic that students often find difficult and confusing and I believe that there are two main reasons for this.

a) The rule of law can be a rather abstract concept and, like other abstract concepts, students often find it difficult to get a definite, firm understanding.

b) There are many different versions of the rule of law and the differences among them can be significant.

I am going to begin with the basic meaning of the rule of law. I strongly advise you to get this basic meaning clear and fixed in your mind. If you do, you will find it much easier to understand some of the different versions of the rule of law that you may meet in your studies.

I will follow this by looking at some different versions of the rule of law.

8.2 The rule of law: basics

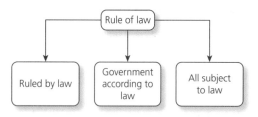

8.2.1 Governed by law

At its most basic, the rule of law simply means that a society is ruled (i.e. governed) by law.

That is, relations among the different people and organisations of a society are administered according to laws.

This might make more sense if we consider some alternatives.

a) In some countries, it may be said that there is a state of lawlessness. This might be because the government has broken down or lost control, say, during or following a revolution or war. Where this is the case, it cannot be said that the rule of law exists. In fact, with regard to such countries, there is often a call for a return to the rule of law – i.e. for the country to be governed by law.

This example helps to illustrate one reason why the rule of law is desirable. An absence of law may also mean that there is an absence of security for persons or property – the rule of law helps to provide that security.

This preference for law rather than anarchy is captured by Bradley and Ewing:

'Law and order [is] better than anarchy.'
(Bradley, A.W. and Ewing, K.D., *Constitutional and Administrative Law*, 15th edn, 2011, London: Longman)

b) Imagine you lived in a society governed by a ruler according to his whim. In such a situation you may not know what was required to avoid sanction or punishment. One day you might be expected to enthusiastically join the ruler's criticism of his in-laws while the same behaviour the next day might see you severely punished for insulting members of his family.

There would not be the rule of law in such a society; you would be governed instead by arbitrariness and caprice.

This preference for the rule of law rather than rule by an individual has been recognised by Aristotle:

'It is better for the law to rule than one of the citizens.'
(Warington, J. (trans. and ed.), *Aristotle's Politics and Athenian Constitution*, 1959, London: J.M. Dent)

It has also been recognised by the US Supreme Court in one of its earliest and most famous cases.

Case:	
***Marbury v Madison* 5 US 137 (1803) 163**	Marshall CJ: *'The government of the United States has been emphatically termed a government of laws, and not of men.'*

8.2.2 Government according to law

Implicit in the idea that we should be ruled by law is the idea that we should be ruled lawfully. That is, we should be governed according to law and the government should act lawfully and be bound by the law.

Rule of Law → means → Ruled lawfully/according to law → means → The government should act lawfully and be bound by the law

The idea that there should be government according to law is considered one of most important aspects of the principle of the rule of law. If the government was not constrained by the law, if it could act unlawfully, then we would have the situation described above (Section 8.2.1) where a country's citizens would be subject to arbitrary rule at the whim of their rulers.

The principle of government according to law can be seen in the following two cases.

Case:	
Entick v Carrington (1765) 19 St Tr 1029	Facts: Entick was suspected of being the author of seditious writings (writings critical of the government). Carrington, the Secretary of State, issued a warrant for the King's men to enter Entick's property and seize his papers. Entick sued for trespass. The Government acknowledged that there had been no legal power to issue the warrant argued that it was necessary that it had such power.
	Held: The absence of legal authority giving the Government the relevant power made their actions an unlawful trespass.
	Lord Camden CJ: *'By the laws of England, every invasion of private property, be it ever so minute, is a trespass. No man can ever set his foot upon my ground without my licence, but he is liable to an action ... If he admits the fact, he is bound to shew by way of justification, that some positive law has empowered or excused him ... And with respect to the argument of State necessity, or a distinction that has been aimed at between State offences and others, the common law does not understand that kind of reasoning, nor do our books take notice of any such distinction.'*

Case:	
M v Home Office [1994] 1 AC 377	Facts: M was deported. A judge ordered the Home Secretary to secure M's return to the UK. The Home Secretary believed the judge did not have jurisdiction to issue such an order against him and so ignored it.
	Held: the Home Secretary was not entitled to ignore the order of the judge.
	Lord Templeman: *'My Lords, the argument that there is no power to enforce the law by injunction or contempt proceedings against a minister in his official capacity would, if upheld, establish the proposition that the executive obey the law as a matter of grace and not as a matter of necessity.'*

8.2.3 The law applies to all

Barnett writes:

'The essence of the rule of law is that of the sovereignty or supremacy of law over man. The rule of law insists that every person – irrespective or rank and status in society – be subject to the law.'

(Barnett, H., *Constitutional and Administrative Law*, 9th edn, 2011, London: Routledge)

A society would not be ruled by law if some people were exempt from the law, perhaps because they belonged to a particular social class or held a particular office.

Imagine, for example, if some people were exempt from the law so that they could take another's property, injure or kill them without fear of punishment. In such a society there would be arbitrariness and caprice: those obliged to act lawfully would be at the mercy of those who were above the law. For many, there would be no security of property or person.

Indeed, a society in which the law applied to some and not to others would be one largely characterised by anarchy rather than one governed by law.

Workpoint

The Vienna Convention on Diplomatic Relations gives diplomats legal immunity from prosecution or civil suit in their host country.
Construct an argument as to why such immunity is legitimate even though it appears to breach the principle of the rule of law that the law should apply to all.

8.2.3.1 Equality before the law

The principle that all are subject to law also suggests that the law should apply equally to all. Indeed, equality before the law is, generally speaking, accepted as implicit in the ideal of the rule of law.

However, it is also accepted that complex societies need to assign different rights and duties to different people.

For example:

• children under the age of ten are conclusively presumed not to be guilty of a criminal offence;

• the police have powers of stop, search and arrest that other citizens do not possess.

Assuming that we can all understand why such differences in treatment are appropriate we can also understand that a basic demand that the law should apply equally to all may be too simplistic. We therefore need a more nuanced principle. I suggest:

The rule of law demands equality before the law or that any differences in treatment are justifiable in some legitimate way.

So, for instance, treating a young child differently than an adult in criminal law is justifiable in a legitimate way because young children do not have the same capacity as adults to know right from wrong or understand the consequences of their actions. In contrast, treating a person differently because of the colour of their skin cannot be legitimately justified and would breach the general principle of equality before the law.

8.3 Different versions of the rule of law

We are going to examine three different versions of the rule of law: by Dicey, Joseph Raz and Lord Bingham.

8.3.1 Dicey's version of the rule of law

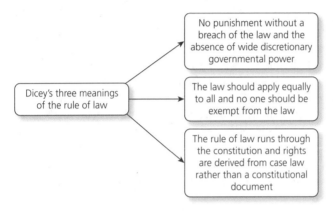

It is inevitable that you will come across Dicey's version of the rule of law, both in your classes and in your own reading. Dicey ascribes three meanings to the rule of law.

a) No one should be punished except for a breach of the law as established in the ordinary courts. The rule of law is against the existence of wide arbitrary or discretionary power on the part of those in authority.

The first part of this first meaning is easily recognisable as an aspect of the rule of law. A society would not be ruled by law if its citizens could be punished even though they had not broken the law. Dicey's requirement that a breach of the law should be established in the 'ordinary courts' helps to guarantee that the law is applied without bias. There may not be this guarantee of impartiality if a special court was set up, and its procedures tailor made, to deal differently with different litigants.

Dicey's rejection of wide arbitrary or discretionary power can be explained as follows: a government body with a large degree of discretion has a lot of flexibility in the way it deals with its citizens. In such a situation, one could not be sure that like cases were being treated alike; indeed, very wide discretion would mean that citizens would not be ruled by ascertainable rules but, rather, by capriciousness and whim – the opposite of the rule of law (see Section 8.2.1 above).

b) The law requires that all should be equally subject to the law as established in the ordinary law courts and that there should be no exemption of officials or others from the law.

This should be familiar from the earlier discussion above (Section 8.2.3) that the law should apply to all and there should be equality before the law.

Dicey's requirement that the law should be established in the ordinary courts deserves closer examination. In essence, his point is that equality before the law might be threatened if different courts existed for different groups of people. If, for instance, cases against the government were dealt with in specialist courts, different from the courts that dealt with cases against ordinary citizens, there would be a danger of these different courts treating similar cases differently. If all cases are dealt with in the same, ordinary courts, using the same procedures and applying the same laws, then this helps to guarantee equality of treatment.

c) The rule of law runs through the UK constitution and constitutional principles (such as the right to liberty) are the result of case law rather than guarantees in some constitutional document or Bill of Rights.

The first thing to keep in mind here is that Dicey is writing long before the European Convention on Human Rights and the Human Rights Act 1998.

In this third meaning of the rule of law, Dicey seems to be celebrating the way in which rights in the UK are traditionally established and protected and denigrating the way countries with constitutional guarantees protect such rights.

His argument seems to be that rights in the UK are more concrete because they are derived from real-life cases in which the courts have proved themselves willing to protect the rights in question. This, he suggests, is worth more than rights contained in a constitutional document that may turn out to be nothing more than empty paper promises.

An example might illustrate his point with regard to constitutional guarantees. Article 35 of the 1982 Constitution of the People's Republic of China states: '*Citizens of the People's Republic of China enjoy freedom of speech, of the press, of assembly, of association, of procession and of demonstration*', yet few outside China (and perhaps few within) would believe that this is a right on which Chinese citizens can always depend.

It is difficult to see why the rule of law should require rights to be derived from case law rather than a constitutional document. Yet, Dicey's point here may be explainable in the following way:

• If the rule of law requires certain rights and principles to be protected (and I should note that some would disagree on this point) then this protection is more likely to occur if the rights in question are derived from case law rather than from a constitution, a bill of rights or similar document.

8.3.2 Raz's version of the rule of law

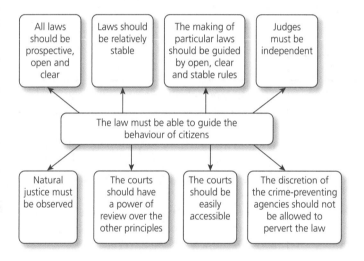

Raz starts with a basic, broad definition of the rule of law:

'It has two aspects: (1) that people should be ruled by the law and obey it, and (2) that the law will be such that people will be able to be guided by it.'

(Raz, J., 'The Rule of Law and Its Virtue' (1977) 93 LQR 195, p. 198)

From this basic idea that the law should be able to guide people's behaviour so that they know what is required of them to act lawfully, he develops eight principles inherent in the rule of law.

a) 'All laws should be prospective, open and clear.'

Laws should not be hidden, secret or unnecessarily opaque. Also, laws should not have retrospective effect.

Workpoint

Read the *Burmah Oil* case and the War Damage Act 1965 in Section 6.4.4. In what way does the War Damage Act 1965 breach this first principle of Raz's?

Workpoint

Consider the following case: *Shaw v DPP*. In what ways does this case breach Raz's first principle?

Case:	
Shaw v DPP [1962] AC 220	Facts: Shaw published a directory giving the contact details of prostitutes and information about the services they offered. Before publication, he consulted a solicitor and Scotland Yard and was informed that it would not be an offence to publish the directory. After publication he was charged with conspiracy to corrupt public morals – something that was not a crime by virtue of statute and there had never been a case where someone had been convicted of the offence.
	Held: The House of Lords was certain that the offence existed and that the courts had a residual power to maintain the moral welfare of the state.

b) *'Laws should be relatively stable.'*

This does not mean that the law should be absolutely fixed and never changing (which is why Raz uses the word 'relatively'). However, the law should be sufficiently stable so that one is able to plan to live one's life lawfully.

c) *'The making of particular laws (particular legal orders) should be guided by open, stable, clear and general rules.'*

Government bodies are often given discretionary powers to make rules and orders governing citizens' lives. These discretionary powers should themselves be guided by open, clear and general rules so that the citizen is able to predict how they will be applied in their situation.

d) *'The independence of the judiciary must be guaranteed.'*

Citizens would not be able to live their lives guided by the law if, when a case came to court, the judge did not decide the case according to law but for some other reason, perhaps because he or she was influenced by bias or pressured by the government to decide the case one way rather than another. It is therefore important that judges are independent and insulated from such pressure. See also Section 5.4.

e) *'The principles of natural justice must be observed.'*

We will look at the principles of natural justice in Chapter 11, section 11.4.2. For now it is sufficient to say that they require hearings to be fair and free from bias. Without this, the law would not be applied impartially and, in a similar way to the rationale for principle (d), citizens could not be sure what was required of them to live lawfully.

f) *'The courts should have review powers over the implementation of the other principles.'*

The courts should have the power to examine the legality of primary and secondary legislation and to review the legality of actions and decisions taken by governmental bodies.

g) *'The courts should be easily accessible.'*

Long delays in court cases or excessive costs may mean that the citizen is not in reality able to make a claim or defend their actions in court. This, in turn, would mean that the law would not be enforced and could not be relied on to guide citizens' behaviour.

Workpoint

Read Section 6.5.7 on ouster clauses. Construct an argument as to why the treatment of such provisions can be explained as the fulfilment of this requirement that the courts should be accessible.

h) *'The discretion of the crime preventing agencies should not be allowed to pervert the law.'*

Discretion is built into the criminal justice system, from a police officer deciding not to take action against a speeding motorist to the Crown Prosecution Service deciding that it would be contrary to the public interest to continue with a prosecution. However, the law would be subverted if this discretion was systematically used to exempt certain people or classes of people from its ambit.

8.3.3 Lord Bingham's version of the rule of law

'The core of the existing principles is, I suggest, that all persons and authorities within the state, whether public or private, should be bound by and entitled to the benefit of laws publicly and prospectively promulgated and publicly administered in the courts. I doubt if anyone would suggest that this statement, even if accurate as one of general principle, could be applied without exception or qualification. There are, for instance, some proceedings in which justice can only be done if they are not in public.'

(Lord Bingham, 'The Rule of Law' [2007] CLJ 67, 69)

Lord Bingham suggests that the rule of law consists of eight sub-rules, many of which are similar to the principles suggested by Raz.

a) *'[T]he law must be accessible and so far as possible intelligible, clear and predictable.'*

b) *'[Q]uestions of legal right and liability should ordinarily be resolved by application of the law and not the exercise of discretion.'*

c) *'[T]he laws of the land should apply equally to all, save to the extent that objective differences justify differentiation.'*

d) *'[T]he law must afford adequate protection of fundamental human rights.'*

e) *'[M]eans must be provided for resolving without prohibitive cost or inordinate delay, bona fide civil disputes which the parties themselves are unable to resolve.'*

f) *'[M]inisters and public officers at all levels must exercise the powers conferred on them reasonably, in good faith, for the purpose for which the powers were conferred and without exceeding the limits of such powers.'*

g) '[A]djudicative procedures provided by the state should be fair.'

h) '[T]he rule of law requires compliance by the state with its obligations in international law ... whether deriving from treaty or international custom or practice [which] governs the conduct of nations.'

> **Workpoint**
>
> Explain how the versions of the rule of law given by Dicey, Raz and Bingham relate to the basic version described in Sections 8.2.1, 8.2.2 and 8.2.3.

> **Workpoint**
>
> Make a list of the similarities and differences among the different versions of the rule of law posited by Dicey, Raz and Bingham.

8.3.4 Procedural and substantive versions of the rule of law

It is possible to distinguish different versions of the rule of law according to whether they are procedural or substantive.

• A procedural version of the rule of law may require the law to be made and applied in a particular way but will make no requirement about the content of the law.

• A substantive version of the rule of law may also make requirements about how the law is created and applied but it will also say something about the content of the law.

So, for instance, a requirement that the laws of a legal system should be enacted in a particular way and published openly (so that people can discover what the law requires) is a procedural requirement. A requirement that a legal system should respect certain human rights is a substantive requirement because it makes a demand about the content of law.

This distinction – procedural or substantive – is also sometimes referred to as 'formal or substantive' or 'thin or thick' versions of the rule of law.

8.4 Parliamentary supremacy and the rule of law

There is a potential conflict between the principle of parliamentary supremacy and the rule of law.

Simply put, the problem is, under the traditional view of parliamentary supremacy, Parliament may enact any law, including one breaching the principles of the rule of law. For instance:

• Parliament may legislate that those of a particular ethnicity must register with, and regularly report to, their local police station. Such legislation would breach the principle of equality before the law or that any differences in treatment are justifiable in some legitimate way (Section 8.2.3.1).

• Parliament could legislate so that serving police officers could not be prosecuted for any criminal offence. This would breach the principle of equality before the law and that government and its officials should be subject to the law.

If Parliament did legislate in either of these ways then, under the traditional view of parliamentary supremacy, the courts could not rule the legislation to be invalid (see Sections 6.4.1 and 6.4.2).

This potential conflict leads some commentators to argue that Parliament's legislative power should be curtailed so that it is unable to legislate in a way that breaches the rule of law.

In response, supporters of the traditional view of parliamentary supremacy argue that there is only an *apparent* conflict between parliamentary supremacy and the rule of law because in reality Parliament would never enact legislation that breaches the principles of the rule of law.

Checklist – The rule of law

Item on checklist:	Done!
I can give a basic, brief definition of the rule of law.	
I can explain what is meant by government according to law.	
I can explain why the rule of law requires everybody to be subject to the law.	
I can give an account of the three meanings that Dicey ascribes to the rule of law.	
I can explain the rationale underpinning the eight principles in Raz's version of the rule of law.	
I can explain the rationale underpinning the eight principles in Lord Bingham's version of the rule of law.	
I can explain why there is a potential conflict between the rule of law and parliamentary supremacy.	

Research Point

Read Lord Bingham's article, 'The Rule of Law' [2007] CLJ 67. Why does he argue that adequate protection must be given to human rights? Do you agree? What is the alternative argument? Lord Bingham also argues that the rule of law requires that those accused of an offence should know the details of the case against them. Why is this necessary?

Research Point

Read P.P. Craig's article, 'Formal and Substantive Conceptions of the Rule of Law: an Analytical Framework' [1997] *Public Law* 466. Summarise the different versions of the rule of law that he describes.

Research Point

Access the website of a quality newspaper. Using its search facility, search for use of the phrase *'the rule of law'*. Explain the context in which the phrase is being used and what the user meant by it.

Potential exam question

Describe and explain the meaning Dicey ascribed to the rule of law.

Chapter 9
The European Union

This chapter will look at the following:

- a brief history and overview of the EU including details of when each member state joined;

- the institutions of the EU and their respective functions;

- sources of EU law;

- the supremacy of EU law and its relevance for UK constitutional law.

9.1 Introduction

European Union law will exist as a separate subject of study for most, if not all, readers of this text. For this reason, this chapter will simply give a basic introduction of some of the main aspects of EU law and the way in which the supremacy of EU law affects the principle of parliamentary sovereignty.

9.2 Overview and brief history

The European Union has been known by other names in the past. It was initially known as the European Economic Community (EEC) or the Common Market. In the 1980s, it became known as the European Community and it is now known as the European Union (EU). It was created by the Treaty of Rome 1957 and came into being on 1 January 1958.

Initially, the EEC had a number of primary aims:

- to create a free trade area between the member states so that trade between them could be undertaken without the normal restrictions that exist between different countries. That is, the EEC sought to enable trade between member states without such things as customs duties or duties or restrictions on import or export between the members of the EEC. To this end, the EEC sought to abolish any-thing that might impede the free movement of people, goods, serv-ices or capital (sometimes referred to as the four freedoms) between member states;

- to adopt common policies in areas such as agriculture, fishing and transport;

- to adopt a common policy with regard to trade with non-member states.

However, it is important to realise that the EU has always been about more than simply facilitating trade between its members. It was born after two devastating world wars, centred on mainland Europe, and was conceived as a way of preventing further wars between the Euro-pean powers by binding them together as members of a European community.

There are 27 members of the EU. The six founding members are: Belgium, France, Germany, Italy, Luxemburg and the Netherlands.

The UK joined in 1972, along with Denmark and Ireland. Greece joined in 1981. Spain and Portugal joined in 1986. In 1995, Austria, Finland and Sweden joined. Ten countries joined the EU in 2004: Cyprus, the Czech Republic, Estonia, Hungary, Latvia, Lithuania, Malta, Poland, the Slovak Republic and Slovenia. In 2007, Bulgaria and Romania became member states.

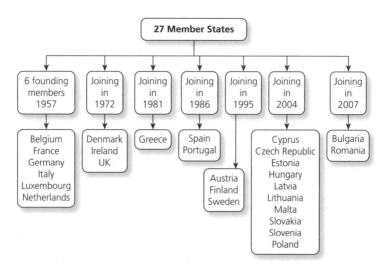

At the time of writing it is expected that Croatia will join the EU in the summer of 2013.

9.3 Institutions of the EU

The main institutions of the EU for our purposes are:

- the European Council
- the Commission
- the Council of the European Union
- the European Parliament
- the Court of Justice of the European Union.

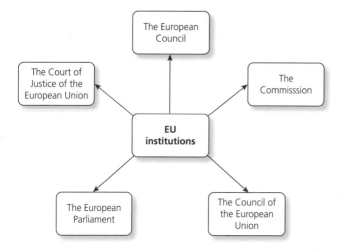

Also, the Treaty of Lisbon 2009 created two new offices:

- the President of the European Council
- High Representative of the Union for Foreign Affairs and Security Policy.

Both are appointed on a vote of the European Council.

The European Council
The European Council is made up of the Heads of Government of the member states along with the President of the European Council and the President of the Commission. It meets about four times a year and its primary role is to set the policy direction for the EU.

The Commission
The Commission is the executive of the EU. It is made up of 27 Commissioners, including the President of the Commission. These are

nominated by each member state but are expected to represent the interests of the EU as a whole. Each Commissioner is assigned an area of responsibility.

The two main roles of the Commission are:

a) to propose legislation to the Parliament and Council of the European Union;

b) to ensure compliance with EU law and ensure that it is implemented and applied (in this role, the Commission is sometimes known as the Guardian of the Treaties).

The Council of the European Union

The Council of the European Union may also be referred to as the Council of Ministers or simply the Council. It is made up of ministers from each member state. Its membership changes according to the matter under consideration. So, for instance, if the matter under discussion is agriculture then the Council will comprise the agriculture ministers of the member states. The members of the Council are expected to represent the interests of their member state so that, for instance, the UK member is expected to represent the interests of the UK.

Its main roles include:

• enacting legislation (usually with the Parliament) that has been proposed by the Commission;

• developing the EU's security and foreign policy.

The European Parliament

There are 754 members of the European Parliament, known as Members of the European Parliament (MEPs), who are directly elected by the citizens of the member states. The number of MEPs each member state has is dependent on the size of its population. MEPs sit in political, rather than geographical, groupings.

The Parliament plays a role in the legislative process, though it is less powerful as a law-maker than the legislatures of most states. In the first place, it cannot initiate legislation itself; this is the role of the Commission. Second, in most cases it cannot pass legislation on its own without the consent of the Council of the European Union.

The Parliament must also approve the appointment of the Commission as a whole and may vote to remove the Commission as a whole. The Parliament also has an oversight role with regard to the EU budget and its approval for the budget must be obtained.

The Court of Justice of the European Union
This was formerly known as the European Court of Justice. It is made up of three courts.

• *The Court of Justice*

  The Court of Justice adjudicates on cases brought by the Commission or member states alleging a breach by another member state of their EU obligations. The Court also rules on questions of EU law that are referred to it by the domestic courts of the member states. In addition, the Court hears appeals from the General Court.

• *The General Court*

  The General Court was formerly known as the Court of First Instance. It mainly deals with cases brought by individuals or corporations alleging illegality on the part of the EU institutions.

• *European Union Civil Service Tribunal*

  The EU Civil Service Tribunal rules on cases between the EU and its civil servants.

9.4 Sources of EU law

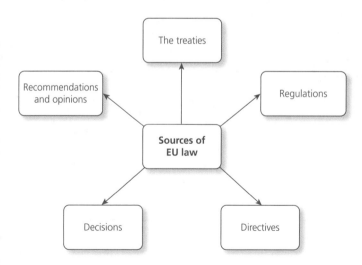

9.4.1 The treaties

The EU is governed by two treaties: the Treaty on European Union (TEU) and the Treaty on the Functioning of the European Union

(TFEU). These two treaties incorporate all the previous treaties (as amended) concerning the operation and institutions of the EU.

The treaties are the primary source of EU law.

9.4.2 Other sources of EU law

Article 288 (TFEU) states:

To exercise the Union's competences, the institutions shall adopt regulations, directives, decisions, recommendations and opinions.

9.4.2.1 Regulations

Article 288 (TFEU) gives the following definition of a regulation:

A regulation shall have general application. It shall be binding in its entirety and directly applicable in all Member States.

Regulations become part of the law of the member states without further legislation or implementation by the member states. This is what is meant by the term *'directly applicable'*.

Also, where a regulation is sufficiently clear and precise, it gives rise to enforceable rights for citizens. In this sense, regulations have direct effect. Such rights are enforceable by citizens against their governments (this is known as vertical effect) and against other citizens or organisations (this is known as horizontal effect).

Definition

Direct applicability: Treaty articles and regulations have direct applicability, which means that they automatically become part of the law of the member states without the need for any further legislation or implementation.
Direct effect: An EU law will have direct effect if it gives rise to rights that are enforceable in the courts of the member states.

At first glance, these two terms 'direct effect' and 'direct applicability' appear to be very similar and students sometimes struggle to differentiate between them. In short, one should remember that a provision of EU law may have direct applicability so that it automatically becomes part of the law of the member states but that its nature or subject matter may be such that it does not give rise to rights that are enforceable in the courts of the member states. If it does give rise to such rights then it will have direct effect.

Direct applicability

The provision automatically becomes part of the law of the member states without the need for legislation or implementation by the member state

Direct effect

The provision gives rise to rights that are enforceable in the courts of the member states

9.4.2.2 Directives

Article 288 (TFEU) states:

A directive shall be binding, as to the result to be achieved, upon each Member State to which it is addressed, but shall leave to the national authorities the choice of form and methods.

A directive will specify an objective, and a date by which that objective has to be achieved, but leave each member state to determine how they might best meet it. In the UK, it will commonly be the case that primary or (more often) secondary legislation is enacted in order to achieve the aims of a directive.

Where a member state fails to implement a directive within the specified time, or implements it only partially or incorrectly, it may still give rise to enforceable rights (i.e. it may have direct effect) if certain conditions are present.

Case:	
***Van Duyn v Home Office* [1974] ECR 1337**	Facts: Van Duyn relied on a directive to challenge a decision excluding her from the UK.
	Held: Directives will have direct effect where the obligations they impose are sufficiently clear and precise and leave no discretion as to the manner of their implementation.

However, generally speaking, directives that have not been sufficiently implemented will give rise only to vertical direct effect; that is, they will be enforceable only against the governments of member states.

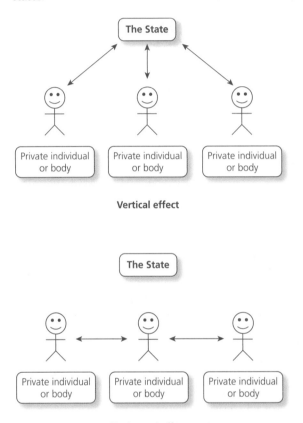

Vertical effect

Horizontal effect

However, the rule that unimplemented directives can only have vertical direct effect is ameliorated slightly, as demonstrated in the following two cases.

Case:	
***Marshall v Southampton Area Health Authority* [1986] ECR 723**	Marshall was able to rely on a directive against her employer because it was a public authority and thus part of the state.

Case:	
***Von Colson v Land Nordrhein-Westfalen* [1984] ECR 1891**	Even in cases between private individuals, the courts of the member states are under an obligation to interpret national law in a way that gives effect to EU law.

The principle at play in the *Von Colson* case is sometimes referred to as incidental (or indirect) horizontal direct effect.

Alternatively, if the directive is such that it does not have direct effect, the member state may be liable for any loss caused by the failure to implement it.

Case:	
***Francovich v Italy* [1991] ECR I-5357**	Facts: Francovich suffered monetary loss as a result of Italy's failure to implement a directive to guarantee payment of outstanding wages should an employer become insolvent.
	Held: A member state may be liable for its failure to fully implement a directive within the specified time if three conditions are present:
	a) the directive creates rights; b) the rights should be ascertainable from the directive; c) there is a causal link between the loss suffered and the failure to implement.

9.4.2.3 Decisions, recommendations and opinions

Article 288 (TFEU) states:

A decision shall be binding in its entirety. A decision which specifies those to whom it is addressed shall be binding only on them.

Recommendations and opinions shall have no binding force.

Decisions are addressed to member states, companies or individuals and are binding on those to whom they are addressed but to no one else.

Recommendations and opinions have no legally binding force.

9.5 The supremacy of EU law

The aspect of EU law that, perhaps, has the most significant consequence for UK constitutional law is the principle that EU law is supreme and takes precedence over any conflicting law of the member states. The supremacy of EU law has been established by the European Court of Justice (now the Court of Justice of the European Union) in a number of cases, including the following two.

Cases:	
NV Algemene Transport – en Expeditie Onderneming Van Gend en Loos v Nederlandse Administratie der Belastingen [1963] ECR 1 (Commonly referred to simply as *Van Gend en Loos*)	The Court stated: *'The … Community constitutes a new legal order of international law for the benefit of which the states have limited their sovereign rights, albeit within limited fields, and the subjects of which comprise not only member states but also their nationals.'*
Costa v ENEL [1964] ECR 585	The Court stated: *'[T]he member states have limited their sovereign rights, albeit within limited fields, and have thus created a body of law which binds both their nationals and themselves … [It is] impossible for the States … to afford precedence to a unilateral and subsequent measure over a legal system accepted by them on a basis of reciprocity … The executive force of Community law cannot vary from one State to another in deference to subsequent domestic laws, without jeopardising the attainment of the objectives of the Treaty … The obligations undertaken under the treaty establishing the Community would not be unconditional, but merely contingent, if they could be called in question by subsequent legislative acts of the signatories.'*

Workpoint

Read the judgment from the *Costa* case, above. Explain why it is necessary for EU law to take precedence over any conflicting law of the member states.

If the UK domestic law conflicts with EU law then the UK courts are under an obligation to give precedence to EU law. This point was made by Lord Denning in the following case.

Case:	
Macarthys v Smith [1979] ICR 785	Lord Denning: *'In construing our statute, we are entitled to look to the Treaty as an aid to its construction, and even more, not only as an aid but as an overriding force. If on close investigation it should appear that our legislation is deficient – or is inconsistent with Community law – by some oversight of our draftsmen – then it is our bounden duty to give priority to Community law.'*

As was discussed in Section 6.5.3, the principle of the supremacy of EU law has implications for the doctrine of parliamentary sovereignty.

Workpoint

Read Section 6.5.3. Explain why the supremacy of EU law might infringe the principle of parliamentary sovereignty. Explain, also, when the UK courts will hold that an Act of Parliament should be applied even if it conflicts with EU law.

Checkpoint – EU law

Item on checklist:	Done!
I can give a brief outline of the initial aims of the EEC (now the EU).	
I know how many states are members of the EU.	

Checkpoint – EU law

Item on checklist:	Done!
I know when the UK joined the EU.	
I can name the principal institutions of the EU and give an account of their primary roles.	
I can identify the different sources of EU law and explain how they differ.	
I know what is meant by the terms *'direct applicability' and 'direct effect'*.	
I can explain why it is considered necessary for EU law to take precedence over any conflicting law of the member states.	
I can explain the effect that the supremacy of EU law has on the UK doctrine of parliamentary sovereignty.	

Potential exam question

With regard to EU law, explain the principles of direct effect and direct applicability and how these apply to treaties, regulations and directives.

Chapter 10
Judicial review 1
Introduction and procedure

In this chapter you will learn:

- the nature of judicial review;
- the remedies available in judicial review;
- when judicial review must be used;
- the time limit for bringing a claim in judicial review;
- who can bring a claim in judicial review.

10.1 Overview of judicial review

Judicial review is procedure by which the courts ensure that those exercising governmental power do so lawfully.

Some examples might illustrate the operation of judicial review.

Let's imagine that an Act of Parliament obliges (the fictional) Ormsborough Council to regulate the operation of its market by issuing licences to those who wish to operate a stall on the market and fining those who attempt to operate a stall without a licence.

The Council is not free to issue licences and fines as it chooses. Like all bodies exercising public power, it must exercise its powers lawfully, fairly and reasonably and if it fails to do so its actions may be challenged by way of judicial review.

For instance, imagine that the Council issues a fine to the local supermarket for operating without a licence. Here, the Council would be acting unlawfully by attempting to use the power it has been given for one purpose, to regulate the Ormsborough market, for a different purpose, to regulate supermarkets. It would have exceeded its power or acted ultra vires. The supermarket could challenge the decision to issue a fine by way of judicial review.

Definition

Ultra vires: Beyond the powers.
Intra vires: Within its powers.

Alternatively, imagine that I apply for a market licence from Ormsborough Council to sell copies of this book. My application is rejected because I do not regularly attend church. I could challenge this decision by way of judicial review on two grounds. First, I could argue that the Council have taken into account an irrelevant consideration, my church attendance, and that they have therefore acted unlawfully by abusing their discretion. Second, I could argue that basing their decision on my church attendance is unreasonable: no reasonable council could have made a decision on this basis.

Finally, imagine that my application for a market licence is refused but no reasons are given. I later find out that the decision was made after the council took evidence from one of my neighbours that I was not a fit and proper person to operate a stall. I might wish to challenge this decision on the ground of procedural impropriety: the procedure used in making the decision was not fair because it was based on evidence about my character that I was given no opportunity to rebut.

These examples give us some indication of the grounds of judicial review, i.e. the reasons that we can use to challenge the actions or decisions of governmental bodies. We will examine the grounds of judicial review in Chapter 11. For now, we can simply note that there are three main grounds:

- illegality (which includes a governmental body exceeding its powers or abusing its discretion);

- irrationality (also known as unreasonableness);

- procedural impropriety.

If a claimant wins her claim for judicial review, the court will grant one or more of a number of remedies, including:

- a quashing order in which the court would quash the decision made; i.e. the decision would be voided, as if it had never been made;

- a mandatory order: the court orders the defendant to act in a particular way;

• a prohibiting order: the court orders the defendant not to act in a particular way;

• a declaration that the action complained of was unlawful.

One important thing to remember about judicial review is that it is not an appeal. The courts do not substitute their decision for that of the defendant (the body exercising the governmental power). Instead, broadly speaking, the courts say that there is some fault with the defendant's decision or action. So, to go back to the above example, I might win my claim for judicial review on the ground that the Council has not followed the correct procedure when refusing me a market licence. As a result, the court might quash the Council's original decision and order it to retake it following an appropriate procedure. The Council might do this and still decide (this time following a fair procedure) not to give me a licence. In other words, it is possible to win a claim for judicial review but not to really win the battle overall.

Claims for judicial review are brought in the Administrative Court, which is part of the High Court.

In this chapter we will look at the following aspects of judicial review:

• the types of decision that may be challenged by judicial review;

• the permission stage;

• the time limit for bringing a claim;

• who can bring a claim (the sufficient interest requirement).

Workpoint

It is often said that judicial review helps to maintain the rule of law (see Chapter 8). Explain how it does this.

10.2 The judicial review jurisdiction

Part 54, rule 1 of the Civil Procedure Rules gives some indication of the scope of judicial review. It states:

a 'claim for judicial review' means a claim to review the lawfulness of–

i) an enactment; or

ii) a decision, action or failure to act in relation to the exercise of a public function.

In brief, judicial review may be used to review the exercise of public power. Such power may be derived from:

- an Act of Parliament or
- the royal prerogative.

Case:	
Council of Civil Service Unions v Minister for the Civil Service [1985] AC 374	Facts: One issue for the court was whether power derived from the royal prerogative was susceptible to judicial review.
	Lord Diplock: *'For a decision to be susceptible to judicial review the decision-maker must be empowered by public law (and not merely, as in arbitration, by agreement between private parties) to make decisions that, if validly made, will lead to administrative action or abstention from action by an authority endowed by law with executive powers ... The ultimate source of the decision-making power is nearly always nowadays a statute or subordinate legislation made under the statute; but in the absence of any statute regulating the subject matter of the decision the source of the decision-making power may still be the common law itself, i.e., that part of the common law that is given by lawyers the label of "the prerogative."'*

Alternatively, the public power in question may not be derived from a legal source but may simply exist (i.e. it may not be derived from legislation or the prerogative):

Case:	
R v Panel on Take-Overs and Mergers, ex parte Datafin [1987] QB 815	Facts: Datafin wanted to challenge a decision made by the Panel on Take-Overs and Mergers, a regulatory body of the Stock Exchange. The power of the Panel was not derived from an Act of Parliament but from the consent of those it regulated and the court had to decide whether it was susceptible to judicial review.
	Held: The court had jurisdiction to judicially review public law power regardless of its source.

The courts will not review private law power, even if that power is exercised by a public (i.e. governmental) body.

There were a number of cases, particularly in the 1980s and 1990s, that attempted to define the limits of the judicial review jurisdiction and various tests were suggested by academics and others for determining whether a particular function was susceptible to review. This issue has largely died down and it is unlikely that you will be tested on it.

The main thing to remember is that the courts' judicial review jurisdiction can be exercised only in respect of public, not private, power. Judicial review is often tested by way of a problem question and, in most assessment questions, it will be obvious that the power in question is public in nature and so susceptible to review; for example, the power may be exercised by a government minister and derived from an Act of Parliament.

> Note: Judicial review cannot be used if the claimant has another avenue available by which they may challenge the decision, e.g. an appeal.

Workpoint

Read Section 6.5.7 on ouster clauses. What effect do such clauses have on the courts' power to review a particular matter?

10.2.1 Procedural exclusivity

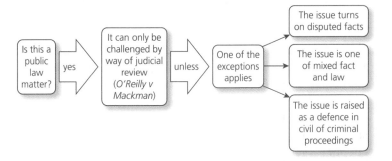

In the preceding section, I noted that judicial review can be used to challenge the exercise of public power. In actual fact, the position is much stronger than this: with a few exceptions, if you wish to challenge the exercise of public power you *must* do so by judicial review. This is known as procedural exclusivity (i.e. judicial review is the exclusive procedure by which public power may be challenged in the courts). It comes from the following case.

Case:	
O'Reilly v Mackman [1983] 2 AC 237	Facts: Prison rioters had been punished by a disciplinary tribunal. They challenged the decisions of the tribunal, arguing that an unfair procedure had been adopted. They brought their challenge by ordinary court action rather than by judicial review.
	Held: The claim was struck out as an abuse of the process of the court; the disciplinary tribunal was exercising a public law function and so its decisions could be challenged only by judicial review.

10.2.1.1 Exceptions to O'Reilly v Mackman

The courts have developed a number of exceptions to the procedural exclusivity rule in the *O'Reilly* case.

a) *Where the matter is one that largely turns on disputed facts*

For a variety of reasons, the judicial review procedure is not the most appropriate forum in which disputed facts may be resolved. So, when facts are in dispute, the courts might consider it appropriate to bring a challenge to the exercise of public power by the ordinary proceedings rather than by way of judicial review.

Case:	
Trustees of the Dennis Rye Pension Fund v Sheffield City Council [1998] 1 WLR 840	Facts: The Council refused to pay improvement grants in respect to properties held by the claimants because repairs carried out on the properties had not been completed to a satisfactory standard.
	Held: Whether the repairs had been carried out to the requisite standard turned largely on issues of fact and so was best resolved in ordinary proceedings rather than by way of judicial review.

b) *When the matter in dispute is a mixture of public and private law*

Case:

| *Roy v Kensington and Chelsea and Westminster Family Practitioner Committee* **[1992] 2 WLR 239** | Facts: Roy was a GP (a doctor). The Family Practitioner Committee refused to pay him the full amount of money that he claimed he was owed. |
| | Held: Roy's relationship with the Committee was contractual, and so a private law matter, even though the distribution of public funds by the Committee was a public law function. Because of this, the matter was a mixture of public and private law and so could be pursued by ordinary proceedings. |

c) *Where the public law matter is raised as a defence in civil or criminal proceedings*

Cases:

Wandsworth London Borough Council v Winder **[1985] AC 461**	Facts: Winder believed the Council had acted unlawfully in raising the rents on council-owned properties (of which he was a tenant) and so he decided not to pay the increased rent. The council brought an action against him for the unpaid rent and he used their alleged illegality (unlawfully raising rents) as his defence. The council applied to have his defence struck out as an abuse of process.
	Held: Winder was not bringing a challenge but was simply alleging illegality as part of his defence in a challenge brought against him. This was not, therefore, an abuse of process.
Boddington v British Transport Police **[1998] 2 WLR 639**	Facts: Boddington was convicted of an offence of smoking a cigarette in a railway carriage. As part of his defence, he attempted to challenge the lawfulness of the bylaw that made smoking on a train an offence.
	Held: The defendant was not precluded from raising a public law matter as part of his defence in a criminal prosecution against him.

10.3 Judicial review pre-action protocol

The pre-action protocol is a code of good practice consisting of steps the parties should follow before litigation. It includes:

• a suggestion that the parties try to resolve the matter other than by litigation, e.g. by alternative dispute resolution;

• a suggestion that the claimant sends the defendant a letter identifying the issues in dispute and seeking to avoid litigation. Defendants should normally reply to the letter within 14 days.

> Note: The pre-action protocol does not affect the time limit by which a claim should be made (see Section 10.5, below).

10.4 Permission stage

The permission stage was formerly known as the leave stage.
Section 31(3) of the Senior Courts Act 1981:

'No application for judicial review shall be made unless the leave of the High Court has been obtained in accordance with rules of court.'

Part 54, rule 4 of the Civil Procedure Rules:

*'54.4 Permission required
The court's permission to proceed is required in a claim for judicial review whether started under this Part or transferred to the Administrative Court.'*

Judicial review is a two-stage process:

• the permission stage

and

• the substantive hearing stage.

The permission stage is simply that. A claimant applies to the court for permission to continue with their claim for judicial review. If the court refuses, then the claim does not proceed. The rationale behind the permission stage is to root out those cases that are weak or unarguable and should not therefore proceed because they have an unrealistic prospect of success.

In most cases, the permission stage will be made without a hearing; the judge will simply consider the claim on the basis of the claim form and the defendant's written response.

10.5 Time limit

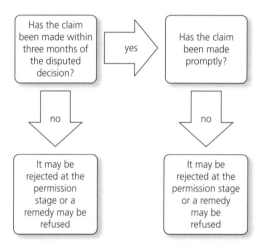

Part 54, rule 5 of the Civil Procedure Rules:

54.5 Time limit for filing claim form

1) *The claim form must be filed –*
    a) *promptly; and*
    b) *in any event not later than 3 months after the grounds to make the claim first arose.*
2) *The time limit in this rule may not be extended by agreement between the parties.*
3) *This rule does not apply when any other enactment specifies a shorter time limit for making the claim for judicial review.*

The time limit for bringing a claim in judicial review is very short:

• a claimant must bring their claim promptly or in any event within three months.

It is important that you realise the courts may still rule that a claim has been made with undue delay, even if brought within three months, if they consider that it has not be made promptly.

Case:	
R v Swale Borough Council, ex parte Royal Society for the Protection of Birds (1990) 2 Admin. L.R. 790	Held: Although the RSPB had brought the claim within three months, it had not acted promptly.

Section 31(6) of the Senior Courts Act 1981:

Where the High Court considers that there has been undue delay in making an application for judicial review, the court may refuse to grant–

a) leave for the making of the application; or
b) any relief sought on the application,

if it considers that the granting of the relief sought would be likely to cause substantial hardship to, or substantially prejudice the rights of, any person or would be detrimental to good administration.

Where the court considers there has been undue delay in making a claim it may refuse permission for the claim to proceed or may allow the claim to proceed but refuse to grant a remedy.

However, the courts may extend the time limit beyond three months where they think there is good reason to do so.

Case:	
R v Dairy Produce Quota Tribunal for England and Wales, ex parte Caswell [1990] 2 AC 738	Facts: Caswell attempted to challenge a decision of the Tribunal approximately three years after it had been made.
	Held: The House of Lords held that the courts had the power to extend the time limit beyond three months where they considered there to be good reason to do so but that in the present case, and given the lapse of time, it would be detrimental to good administration to grant the remedy sought.

10.6 Sufficient interest

Section 31(3) of the Senior Courts Act 1981:

[T]he court shall not grant leave to make such an application [for judicial review] unless it considers that the applicant has a sufficient interest in the matter to which the application relates.

Section 31(3) of the Senior Courts Act 1981 requires a claimant to have sufficient interest in the claim before it will be allowed to proceed. The sufficient interest requirement is sometimes known as the requirement that a claimant has 'standing' or (in older cases) '*locus standi*'. The rationale of the sufficient interest requirement is to filter out busybodies, trouble-makers or cranks.

A return to our example from the beginning of the chapter might illustrate its function. Imagine that my application for a licence to operate a stall on Ormsborough market is refused for one of the reasons given in Section 10.1. Also imagine that I decide not to take the matter further but my neighbour, Mr Meddler, is offended at the way I have been treated and decides to bring a claim in judicial review on my behalf. The court would prevent his claim proceeding beyond the permission stage on the basis that he did not have sufficient interest in the matter.

At one time, a claimant would not have sufficient interest to mount a challenge unless he or she had a direct pecuniary (money) interest or an interest over and above the rest of the public. However, the courts have developed a more liberal attitude to standing, beginning with the following case.

Case:	
***Inland Revenue Commissioners v National Federation of Self-Employed and Small Businesses Ltd* [1982] AC 617** (Also known as the Fleet Street Casuals or Mickey Mouse Case)	Facts: Casual print workers in Fleet Street would commonly sign in for work using a false name (e.g. Mickey Mouse) in order to avoid paying tax on their earnings. The Inland Revenue Commission came to an agreement with the employers and unions that, if tax began to be deducted at source, there would be no investigation into failures to pay tax in previous years. The National Federation of Self-Employed and Small Businesses wanted to challenge the lawfulness of this arrangement by way of judicial review. One issue for the court was whether the Federation had sufficient interest.

Held:

- The Federation did not have sufficient interest to challenge the decision.
- Generally speaking, one taxpayer would not have sufficient interest to challenge tax decisions relating to another tax payer.
- A group of individuals who do not have sufficient interest as individuals cannot attain sufficient interest by forming a group or corporation.
- If it is obvious that a claimant does not have sufficient interest, then this should be dealt with at the permission stage; if it is not obvious then the claim should be allowed to proceed to full hearing and the sufficient interest issue examined again in the legal and factual context of the case.

It is the last point in the above case that is the most important. It has come to mean that, unless a claimant is obviously a busybody or motivated by malice or ill will, the case will be allowed to proceed to the substantive hearing where the claimant's interest will be examined in the light of the merits of the case.

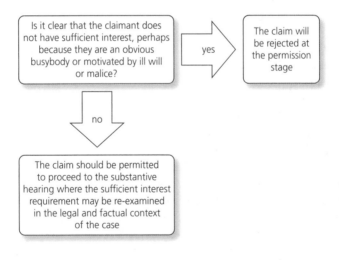

Wade and Forsyth write:

'[The real question is whether the applicant can show some substantial default or abuse, and not whether his personal rights or interests are involved.'
(Wade, H.W.R. and Forsyth, C.F., *Administrative Law*, 10th edn, 2009, Oxford: Oxford University Press)

It is worth noting some other cases in which the relaxed approach to the sufficient interest requirement has been apparent.

Cases:	
***R v HM Treasury, ex parte Smedley* [1985] QB 657**	Facts: Smedley wished to challenge the payment of a sum of money by the UK Government to meet its EC (now EU) obligations. Smedley was not able to show any special interest over and above other taxpayers.
	Held: Smedley lost the case on the substantive issue but the court found that he had sufficient interest to bring the challenge.
	Slade LJ: *'I do not feel much doubt that Mr. Smedley, if only in his capacity as a taxpayer, has sufficient locus standi to raise this question by way of an application for judicial review.'*
***R v Secretary of State for Foreign and Commonwealth Affairs, ex parte Rees-Mogg* [1994] 1 All ER 457**	Facts: Rees-Mogg wanted to challenge the Government's ratification of the Treaty on European Union.
	Held: Rees-Mogg lost the case on the substantive issues but the court held that he had sufficient interest.
	Lloyd LJ: *'There is no dispute as to the applicant's locus standi ... we accept without question that Lord Rees-Mogg brings the proceedings because of his sincere concern for constitutional issues.'*

Cases:	
***R v Inspectorate of Pollution, ex parte Greenpeace (No. 2)* [1994] 4 All ER 329**	Facts: Greenpeace wished to challenge the granting of a licence permitting the testing of a new nuclear processing plant. Held: Greenpeace lost the challenge but the court held that it had sufficient interest, taking the following considerations into account: • Greenpeace was a responsible and respected body with a genuine interest in the issues raised; • it is an organisation of national and international standing and integrity; • the organisation has 2,500 members in the area who might not otherwise have an effective means of bringing their concerns before the court if Greenpeace were denied standing; • if Greenpeace were denied standing, it is likely that there could only be a challenge by an individual and they would not be as well-informed and resourced as Greenpeace. Thus, the court's resources would be stretched. Further, an individual applicant may be financed by legal aid which would leave the defendants without an effective remedy in costs if the applicant lost the case. Also, the organisation has access to scientific, technical and legal expertise that would not be available to the individual applicant.
***R v Secretary of State for Foreign Affairs, ex parte World Development Movement* [1995] 1 All ER 611**	Facts: The World Development Movement (WDM) challenged a grant of money to the Malaysian Government to build a hydro-electric dam. Held: The grant was unlawful. In finding that the WDM had sufficient interest to bring the claim, the court took into account: • the importance of maintaining the rule of law and the importance of the issue raised; • it was unlikely that there would be another responsible challenger; • the WDM had a prominent role in the giving of advice, guidance and assistance regarding aid.

Summary

- Permission should be refused at the permission stage if the claimant obviously does not have sufficient interest – perhaps because they are a mere busybody. Otherwise, the courts will assess the claimant's interest at the substantive hearing and a claimant who raises a valid legal or factual issue will not be found to be lacking interest.

- The courts are unlikely to find an absence of sufficient interest where an individual raises a genuine concern of potentially unlawful government action unless the claimant is motivated by ill will or malice.

- The reputation, expertise and resources of the body bringing the challenge may be a relevant factor in deciding whether it has sufficient interest.

- The likely absence of another responsible, or well-resourced, claimant may be a relevant factor when deciding whether a claimant has sufficient interest.

- The courts will be keen to ensure that unlawful government action does not go unchecked.

Checklist – Judicial review: introduction and procedure

Item on checklist:	Done!
I can give a brief description of what judicial review is.	
I know what remedies are available in judicial review.	
I know what type of power is susceptible to judicial review.	
I know the rule from *O'Reilly v Mackman* and what the exceptions to this rule are.	
I know what the permission stage is for.	
I know the time limit for bringing a claim in judicial review.	
I can explain the sufficient interest requirement and how it operates.	

Research Point

Read the judgment of Sedley J in *R v Somerset County Council, ex parte Dixon* [1998] Env LR 111.

In it, he gives an account of the history of the sufficient interest requirement and of how the courts have arrived at the present position. From this, make your own notes describing the development of the sufficient interest test.

Potential exam question

Explain the operation of the permission stage, the time limit and the sufficient interest requirement in judicial review.

Chapter 11
Judicial review 2
Grounds for judicial review

In this chapter you will learn about the grounds of judicial review, including:

- the three main grounds for judicial review;
- the meaning of illegality and abuse of discretionary power;
- the meaning of irrationality/unreasonableness;
- the meaning of procedural impropriety;
- the rules of natural justice;
- the requirements of fairness;
- the rule against bias;
- legitimate expectation.

11.1 Introduction

The grounds for judicial review are those things that would give rise to a claim for judicial review. There are three grounds of judicial review: illegality, irrationality and procedural impropriety.

These three grounds derive from the following case:

Case:	
Council of Civil Service Unions v Minister for the Civil Service [1985] AC 374	Lord Diplock: *'[O]ne can conveniently classify under three heads the grounds upon which administrative action is subject to control by judicial review. The first ground I would call "illegality," the second "irrationality" and the third "procedural impropriety." '*

> Note:
> * The three grounds of review are convenient headings; as we will see, they encompass a number of sub-grounds.
> * A particular act may be unlawful under more than one ground of review; for instance, an action may be procedurally improper and irrational.

11.2 Illegality

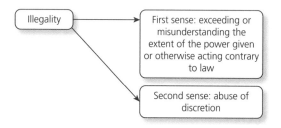

Lord Diplock:

'By "illegality" as a ground for judicial review I mean that the decision-maker must understand correctly the law that regulates his decision-making power and must give effect to it.'

(*Council of Civil Service Unions v Minister for the Civil Service* [1985] AC 374)

It is useful to divide illegality, as a ground of judicial review, into two broad meanings (which can also be sub-divided again, see below):

* illegality in the first sense – where the body exercising the public power exceeds its power, misunderstands the extent or its power or otherwise acts contrary to what is required of it by law;

• illegality in the second sense – where the body exercising the public power abuses its discretion.

11.2.1 Illegality in the first sense: exceeding or misunderstanding the extent of the power given

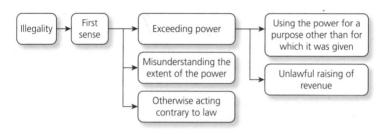

Those exercising public power will act illegally if they:

• exceed the power given, for instance
  • by using it for a purpose other than that for which it was given
  • by attempting to raise revenue without lawful authority;

• misunderstand the extent of their power;

• otherwise act contrary to law.

11.2.1.1 Exceeding power

A body will exceed its power if it uses it for a purpose other than for which it was given.

Case:	
Attorney-General v Fulham Corporation [1921] 1 Ch 440	Facts: The Corporation was given the power by an Act of Parliament to provide facilities for people to wash their clothes. The Corporation used this power to set up a laundry service (i.e. where people's clothes could be left to be washed).
	Held: There was no legal authority to establish a laundry service and so the Corporation exceeded its powers.

A public body will act illegally if it attempts to raise money without lawful authority because this will be viewed as unlawful taxation.

Cases:	
Congreve v Home Office [1976] QB 629	Facts: Some people renewed their television licences earlier than necessary in order to avoid an increase in the television licence fee. The Home Office wrote to these people stating that their licences would be revoked unless they paid an extra £6. Held: The threat to revoke the licences was unlawful; in effect, the Home Office was attempting to levy money without the authority of Parliament.
Woolwich Equitable Building Society v Inland Revenue Commissioners [1993]AC 70	Facts: The Inland Revenue Commission (IRC) had previously been ordered to return to the claimant money that had been unlawfully collected as tax. The IRC returned the money with some, but not all, of the interest. The claimant sued for the remainder of the interest. Held: the remainder of the interest should be paid. Lord Goff: *'the retention by the state of taxes unlawfully exacted is particularly obnoxious, because it is one of the most fundamental principles of our law – enshrined in a famous constitutional document, the Bill of Rights 1688 – that taxes should not be levied without the authority of Parliament; and full effect can only be given to that principle if the return of taxes exacted under an unlawful demand can be enforced as a matter of right.'*

Case:	
R (Shields) v Secretary of State for Justice [2008] EWHC 3102	Facts: Shields had been convicted of attempted murder in Bulgaria. He served part of his sentence in Bulgaria and returned to the UK to serve the remainder. He asked the Justice Secretary to exercise the royal prerogative of mercy and grant a pardon. The Justice Secretary declined on the basis that he was precluded from granting a pardon in such cases.
	Held: The claim for judicial review was allowed; the Justice Secretary was not precluded from granting a pardon in cases such as this.

Ultra vires

We saw in Chapter 10 (Section 10.1) that ultra vires means acting beyond the powers. For instance, it may be used to describe situations such as in the *Attorney-General v Fulham Corporation* case where a body has, using language naturally, gone beyond its powers. However, it may also be used in a more broad sense to refer to any unlawful exercise of public power, whether because of illegality, irrationality or procedural impropriety. For instance, in the *Shields* case, we would not normally say that the Secretary of State for Justice had gone beyond his power when, in actual fact, he failed to appreciate its extent. Yet, it might still be said here that he acted ultra vires.

11.2.1.3 Otherwise acting contrary to law

A public body may also be held to be acting illegally if it acts contrary to its legal requirements in any way. Two ways in which this may happen are if the body acts contrary to the requirements of EU law or if it breaches the Convention rights, i.e. those rights protected by the European Convention on Human Rights. In the latter case, under s 6(1) of the Human Rights Act 1998, a public authority will act illegally if it acts in a way that is incompatible with a Convention right.

We will look in more detail at the operation of this aspect of the Human Rights Act in Chapter 12.

11.2.2 Illegality in the second sense: abuse of discretion

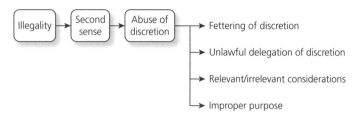

Those exercising public power will act illegally if they abuse their discretion by acting contrary to a number of rules developed by the courts governing the use of discretionary public power. The following are the most prominent examples of an abuse of discretion.

11.2.2.1 Fettering of discretion

Those exercising a discretionary public power would be fettering their discretion if they adopt a hard-and-fast rule that all cases of a particular type will be decided one way rather than another. A decision-maker may adopt a policy where they decide that, in the normal course of events, cases of a particular type will be decided one way rather than another as long as they are prepared to depart from that policy in appropriate cases.

Case:	
***British Oxygen Co. Ltd v Minister of Technology* [1970] AC 610**	Facts: The minister was given a discretionary power to grant money to businesses investing in new technology or plant. He adopted a policy of not awarding a grant for items costing less than £25. British Oxygen was refused a grant for gas cylinders costing £20 each and challenged the decision on the ground that the minister had fettered his discretion.
	Held: The minister had not fettered his discretion because he was willing to consider the merits of each application.
	Lord Reid: *'The general rule is that anyone who has to exercise a statutory discretion must not "shut [his] ears to the application" ... There can be no objection to [adopting a policy] provided the authority is always willing to listen to anyone with something new to say.'*

Case:	
Regina v Secretary of State for the Home Department, ex parte Venables and Thompson [1998] AC 407	Lord Browne-Wilkinson: *'When Parliament confers a discretionary power ... [it] must be exercised on each occasion in the light of the circumstances at that time. In consequence, the person on whom the power is conferred cannot fetter the future exercise of his discretion by committing himself now as to the way in which he will exercise his power in the future ... By the same token, [he] cannot fetter the way he will use that power by ruling out of consideration on the future exercise of that power factors which may then be relevant to such exercise.* *'These considerations do not preclude the person on whom the power is conferred from developing and applying a policy as to the approach which he will adopt in the generality of cases ... But the position is different if the policy adopted is such as to preclude the person on whom the power is conferred from departing from the policy or from taking into account circumstances which are relevant to the particular case in relation to which the discretion is being exercised. If such an inflexible and invariable policy is adopted, both the policy and the decisions taken pursuant to it will be unlawful.'*

11.2.2.2 Unlawful delegation of discretion

Generally speaking, when a discretionary public power is conferred on one body, it will be unlawful for that body to delegate its exercise to another.

Case:	
Vine v National Dock Labour Board [1957] AC 488	Facts: The Dock Workers (Regulation of Employment) Order, 1947 gave the National Dock Labour Board the power to discipline or terminate the employment of dock workers. The Board established a disciplinary committee to carry out this function and this committee terminated the employment of Vine.
	Held: The termination of Vine's employment was invalid; the Board had no authority to delegate its disciplinary power to another body.

However, some delegations of power will be assumed to have been intended by Parliament.

Case:	
Carltona Ltd v Commissioners of Works [1943] 2 All ER 560	Facts: In the Second World War, a minister was given power by the Defence (General) Regulations 1939 to take possession of property if this was considered necessary in the national interest. An order was made requisitioning Carltona's property. Carltona challenged the order on the basis that it had been signed by an official in the Ministry of Works rather than by the minister himself and that it therefore amounted to an unlawful delegation of power.
	Held: The delegation was not unlawful. Parliament could not possibly intend that ministers personally exercise all the powers they are given; rather, Parliament must usually intend that such powers be exercised on the minister's behalf by his officials though the minister remains constitutionally accountable to Parliament with regard to them.

11.2.2.3 Relevant/irrelevant considerations

A decision-maker must take into account all relevant considerations and discount all irrelevant considerations. What is relevant or irrelevant may be governed by statute.

The following case was decided one way at first instance, the court deciding that the defendants had taken into account an irrelevant consideration, and reversed on appeal where the court decided that the defendants had failed to take account of a relevant consideration.

Case:	
R v Somerset County Council, ex parte Fewings [1995] 1 WLR 1037	Facts: An Act of Parliament enabled local authorities to acquire and manage land for the *'benefit, improvement or development of their area'*. The Council voted to ban deer hunting on land acquired under the Act despite a report recommending that hunting was the best way to

manage the deer herd. Those councillors who had voted for the ban on hunting had done so because of the cruelty argument.

Held (first instance): The council was only entitled to ban hunting if it was the best way of managing the herd; banning hunting because of the perceived cruelty was taking into account an irrelevant consideration and was therefore unlawful.

Held (on appeal): The cruelty argument was not necessarily irrelevant when considering the best way to manage the land; however, there was no evidence that the council had considered whether banning hunting was the best way to manage the land, as required under the Act, and so they had failed to take account of a relevant consideration.

11.2.2.4 Improper purpose

When an Act of Parliament grants a discretionary public power, the courts assume that Parliament intends the power to be exercised in accordance with the overall policy and objects of the Act.

Case:	
Padfield v Minister of Agriculture [1968] 2 WLR 92	Facts: A milk-marketing scheme was established by an Act of Parliament which also established an investigation and complaints procedure. The minister refused to refer a complaint to the investigation committee on the ground that it might bring into question the way the scheme as a whole operated.
	Held: The minister acted unlawfully in refusing to refer the complaint; the purpose of an investigation and complaints procedure was to bring into question the way the scheme operated and to refuse to refer a complaint because it might do this was to act contrary to the policy and objects of the Act.

	Lord Reid: *'Parliament must have conferred the discretion with the intention that it should be used to promote the policy and objects of the Act; the policy and objects of the Act must be determined by construing the Act as a whole … [I]f the Minister, by reason of his having misconstrued the Act or for any other reason, so uses his discretion as to thwart or run counter to the policy and objects of the Act, then our law would be very defective if persons aggrieved were not entitled to the protection of the court.'*

Those exercising public power will also be found to have acted with improper purpose, and so illegally, if they exercise it maliciously or in bad faith:

Case:	
Wheeler v Leicester City Council [1985] AC 1054	Facts: Three members of a local rugby club were picked to represent England in a tour of South Africa during the apartheid regime. Leicester CC was opposed to the policy of apartheid and asked the club to condemn the tour. The club stated that it had no power to prevent the players taking part in the tour. The council responded by banning the club from training on council-owned property for 12 months.
	Held: The council had misused its statutory powers (with respect to council-owned land) to punish the club when it had done no wrong.

Checkpoint – Grounds of review in general and illegality

Item on checklist:	Done!
I can name the three grounds of review identified by Lord Diplock in *Council of Civil Service Unions v Minister for the Civil Service*.	
I can give case law authority for the principle that those exercising public power should not exceed that power.	

Item on checklist:	Done!
I can give case law authority for the principle that public bodies should not attempt to raise revenue without the express authorisation of Parliament.	
I can explain the facts and principle of *R (Shields) v Secretary of State for Justice*.	
I can explain the concept of fettering of discretion and give case law authority.	
I can explain the concept of unlawful delegation of discretion and give case law authority.	
I can explain the facts and principle of *Carltona Ltd v Commissioners of Works*.	
I can explain the concept of taking into account an irrelevant consideration or failing to take into account a relevant consideration.	
I can explain what is meant by the concept of using public power for an improper purpose and give examples.	

11.3 Irrationality/ unreasonableness

Lord Diplock:

'By "irrationality" I mean what can by now be succinctly referred to as "Wednesbury unreasonableness" ... It applies to a decision which is so outrageous in its defiance of logic or of accepted moral standards that no sensible person who had applied his mind to the question to be decided could have arrived at it.'

(*Council of Civil Service Unions v Minister of the Civil Service* [1985] AC 374)

'Irrationality' and 'unreasonableness' are used synonymously and interchangeably to refer to decisions that are so absurd they cannot be considered lawful.

The most famous formulation of reasonableness comes from the *Wednesbury* case:

Case:	
Associated Provincial Picture Houses Ltd v Wednesbury Corporation [1948] 1 KB 223	Lord Greene MR: *'[I]f a decision on a competent matter is so unreasonable that no reasonable authority could ever have come to it, then the courts can interfere.'*

Note: In the *Wednesbury* case, Lord Greene used 'unreasonableness' in two ways:

a) in the narrow sense: a decision that is so unreasonable no reasonable body could have made it;

b) to refer to situations that we would now categorise as illegality, such as a decision-maker misdirecting himself in law, taking into account irrelevant considerations or failing to take into account relevant considerations.

In real life, it is very rare that those exercising public power exercise it so unreasonably that no reasonable body could have exercised it in that way. That does not mean, though, that the issue of unreasonableness will not arise in an exam question.

11.3.1 Proportionality

An action will be disproportionate if it is not proportionate to the objective it seeks to achieve. For instance, if the police engaged in a 24-hour surveillance operation in an attempt to catch someone committing a very minor crime then the infringement of the suspect's privacy would be disproportionate to the objective: to detect a minor crime. It is sometimes said that proportionality can be characterised as using a sledgehammer to crack a nut.

Proportionality is a principle in the law of many European countries and is part of EU law and the European Convention on Human Rights. It will therefore come into play in judicial review when an issue of EU law, or under the Human Rights Act 1998 (see Section 11.2.1.3, above), arises. However, outside these areas of law, it is not considered a ground of judicial review.

Proportionality and unreasonableness are closely related: to some degree, each assesses the merits of the decision (i.e. whether it was good or bad). However, the threshold for unreasonableness is much higher than that of proportionality (i.e. it is more difficult to establish unreasonableness than proportionality). Can you articulate why this is the case?

Checkpoint – Irrationality/reasonableness and proportionality

Item on checklist:	Done!
I can give a definition of unreasonableness.	
I can recount Lord Diplock's definition of irrationality.	
I can explain proportionality and the situations in which it may be argued.	

11.4 Procedural impropriety

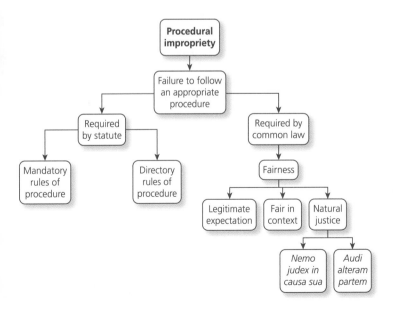

Lord Diplock:

'I have described the third head as "procedural impropriety" rather than failure to observe basic rules of natural justice or failure to act with procedural fairness towards the person who will be affected by the decision. This is because susceptibility to judicial review under this head covers also failure by an administrative tribunal to observe procedural rules that are expressly laid down in the legislative instrument by which its jurisdiction is conferred, even where such failure does not involve any denial of natural justice.'

(*Council of Civil Service Unions v Minister of the Civil Service* [1985] AC 374)

A body exercising public power acts with procedural impropriety if it fails to follow an appropriate procedure as required by statute or the common law.

11.4.1 Procedure required by statute

An Act of Parliament giving a body a public power may specify certain procedural requirements that should be met in the exercise of that power. For instance, it may require that, before a decision is made, the body should:

• consult with certain parties, or

• give notice of a decision in a particular way (e.g. notice in a local newspaper), or

• notify those affected of a right to appeal.

Such procedural requirements may be mandatory or directory. Where mandatory procedural rules are not followed then this will invalidate a decision. If a directory procedural requirement is not followed then this will not necessarily invalidate the decision.

Whether a statutory procedural requirement is considered mandatory or directory will depend on

• the words used in the legislation – words such as 'must' or 'shall' are more likely to make a procedural requirement mandatory;

• whether any substantial hardship is likely to follow if the requirement is not followed.

Case:	
***Agricultural, Horticultural and Forestry Training Board v Aylesbury Mushrooms Ltd* [1972] 1 All ER 280**	Facts: The minister failed to consult a group of mushroom growers, as he was required to do by statute, before initiating a training scheme that required those affected to contribute a levy. Held: Those who had not been consulted did not have to contribute to the levy.

If consultation is required, it must be a genuine invitation to contribute to the decision-making process.

Case:	
***R v Secretary of State for Social Services, ex parte Association of Metropolitan Authorities* [1986] 1 All ER 164**	Facts: The Social Services Secretary had the power to alter a benefits scheme but was obliged by statute to consult representative organisations. The Association of Metropolitan Authorities (AMA) were written to asking for their views but given only a few days to respond. The AMA complained that the consultation requirement had not been complied with. Held: The Secretary of state had failed in his statutory duty to consult. Webster J: *'[T]he essence of consultation is the communication of a genuine invitation to give advice and a genuine receipt of that advice. In my view it must go without saying that to achieve consultation sufficient information must be supplied by the consulting to the consulted party to enable it to tender helpful advice. Sufficient time must be given by the consulting to the consulted party to enable it to do that, and sufficient time must be available for such advice to be considered by the consulting party.'*

11.4.2 Procedure required by common law: natural justice and fairness

The common law procedural requirements are sometimes referred to as the rules of natural justice or, in modern times, the duty to act fairly. These two terms are sometimes used synonymously, though in actual fact the duty to act fairly is wider than, and encompasses, the rules of natural justice.

There are two broad rules of natural justice.

- *Audi alteram partem* (hear the other side): those affected by a decision should be given a chance to influence the decision-making process, to put their case. This rule is sometimes referred to as the right to a fair hearing.

- *Nemo judex in causa sua* (no man a judge in his own cause): those exercising a decision-making power should be free from bias.

The duty to act fairly encompasses the rules of natural justice and *may* also require one or more of the following:

- those affected by a decision are permitted to make representations – written or oral depending on the situation;

- those affected by a decision are informed of the case against them;

- those affected be given an adequate chance to prepare their case;

- those affected by a decision are given a chance to cross-examine witnesses;

- those affected by a decision are entitled to legal representation;

- that reasons are given for a decision.

Precisely what fairness requires in any particular case depends upon context, circumstances and the seriousness of the consequences for those affected by it.

Case:	
***R v Secretary of State for the Home Department, ex parte Doody and Others* [1993] 3 WLR 154**	Lord Mustill: *'[This] is essentially an intuitive judgment.... The standards of fairness are not immutable. They may change with the passage of time, both in general and in their application to decisions of a particular type.... The principles of fairness are not to be applied by rote identically in every situation. What fairness demands is dependent on the context of the decision, and this is to be taken into account in all its aspects.'*

So, in the *Doody* case, Lord Mustill states that the requirements of fairness will be different from case to case and determining what is required in any particular case is essentially an intuitive decision.

The following two cases are very well known and give some idea of the requirements of fairness in different situations.

Cases:	
***Ridge v Baldwin* [1964] AC 40**	Facts: Ridge was a Chief Constable. He had been tried for, and acquitted of, a crime. The local watch committee, responsible for disciplinary issues regarding senior police officers, dismissed him. Ridge had not been present at the meeting where this decision had been taken; he had not been informed of the proposal to dismiss him; he had not been given the details of the case before him; and he had not been given an opportunity to present his case.
	Held: The Watch Committee had acted unlawfully. The rules of natural justice would require him to have been informed of the grounds of the charges against him and given an opportunity to present his case and, because these things did not happen, the decision to dismiss him was null and void.
***McInnes v Onslow-Fane* [1978] 1 WLR 1520**	Note: This is a private law case but the principles derived from it are relevant in the context of judicial review.
	Facts: McInnes applied to the British Boxing Board of Control for a boxers' manager's licence. When making his application, he asked for an oral hearing and prior notification of anything that might prevent the licence being given. The licence was refused and he sought a declaration that the Board had acted in breach of natural justice.
	Held: As this was merely an application for a licence, the Board were simply under a duty to consider it honestly and without bias. The judge distinguished among three categories of case: forfeiture cases, mere applicant cases and renewal cases.

A forfeiture case would be one where the holder's licence was being revoked. In such cases there was a right to an unbiased tribunal, notice of the reasons for the proposed revocation and the right to be heard.

In a mere applicant case, such as McInnes's, there was rarely a right to be heard because one was seeking a privilege rather than defending a charge.

A renewal case was closer to the forfeiture case than the applicant case.

11.4.2.1 The rule against bias

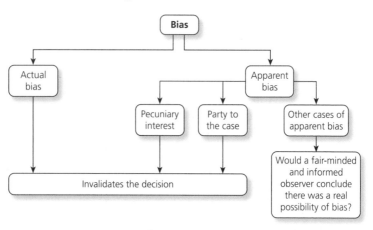

The rule against bias is sometimes referred to as *nemo judex in causa sua* or 'no man a judge in his own cause'. In essence the rule requires that those who have something to gain or lose from a decision, or who may otherwise appear less than impartial, should not make the decision.

If the decision-maker is actually biased, then this will invalidate the decision made. However, it will rarely be possible to establish actual bias (because we cannot see into people's minds) and so we are often talking about whether the appearance of bias is such that the decision should be invalidated.

Apparent bias – pecuniary interest
An apparent bias arising because the decision-maker has a direct pecuniary (i.e. financial) interest in the decision will usually automatically disqualify it.

Case:	
***Dimes v Grand Junction Canal Proprietors* [1852] 3 HL Cas 759**	Facts: The Lord Chancellor, Lord Cottenham, adjudicated on matters involving the canal's proprietors. It was later discovered that he held shares in the company, directly and as a trustee.
	Held: His decisions should be set aside because of his pecuniary interest.
	Lord Campbell: *'No on can suppose that Lord Cottenham could be, in the remotest degree, influenced by the interest that he had in this concern; but, my Lords, it is of the last importance that the maxim that no man is to be a judge in his own cause should be held sacred.'*

Apparent bias – party to the case
If a decision-maker is a party to the case, or has a personal or professional relationship with a party to the case, then that will usually automatically disqualify the decision made.

Cases:	
***R v Sussex Justices, ex parte McCarthy* [1924] 1 KB 256**	Facts: A solicitor representing a client in a civil case against McCarthy also acted as a clerk to the justices in a criminal case against him on the same matter. The clerk retired with the justices when they went to consider their verdict. McCarthy was convicted.
	Held: The conviction was quashed because of an apparent bias.
	Lord Hewart CJ: *'[It] is of fundamental importance that justice should not only be done, but should manifestly and undoubtedly be seen to be done.'*
***R v Bow Street Metropolitan Stipendiary Magistrate and others, ex parte Pinochet Ugarte (No. 2)* [2000] 1 AC 119**	Facts: The Appellate Committee of the House of Lords held that Pinochet should be extradited to Spain to face trial for acts committed when he was President of Chile. Amnesty International had been represented in the case and had argued for extradition. It was later discovered that one of the Law Lords hearing the case, Lord Hoffmann, was a director of Amnesty International Charity.

	Held: The House of Lords set aside its decision.
	Lord Browne-Wilkinson: *'The fundamental principle ... that a man may not be a judge in his own cause ... has two very similar but not identical implications. First it may be applied literally: if a judge is in fact a party to the litigation or has a financial or proprietary interest in its outcome then he is indeed sitting as a judge in his own cause ... [which will lead to] his automatic disqualification. The second application of the principle is where a judge is not a party to the suit and does not have a financial interest in its outcome, but in some other way his conduct or behaviour may give rise to a suspicion that he is not impartial, for example because of his friendship with a party.'*

Test for bias

In cases where the apparent bias will not automatically invalidate a decision, the question arises as to how we determine whether the appearance of bias is such that the decision in question should be nullified.

Case:	
Porter v Magill [2002] 2 AC 357	Lord Hope: *'The question is whether the fair-minded and informed observer, having considered the facts, would conclude that there was a real possibility that the tribunal was biased.'*

11.4.2.2 Legitimate expectation

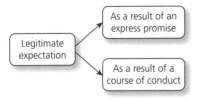

If a body exercising public power engenders a belief that it will be exercised in a particular way then the courts may prevent that body from exercising its power in a different way. Such a belief or legitimate expectation may arise in two ways:

a) either because of an express promise or

b) because of a previous course of action.

That is, the courts recognise that it may be unfair for those exercising public power to disappoint a legitimate expectation that it will be exercised in a particular manner. Such a legitimate expectation may arise through a promise given, or a previous course of action followed, by the body exercising the power.

A legitimate expectation as a result of an express promise

Case:	
***R v Secretary of State for the Home Department, ex parte Khan* [1985] 2 AC 629**	Facts: The Home Office published the criteria that it would use when people in the UK wanted to adopt a child from abroad. Khan applied for an entrance clearance certificate for a child he wished to adopt. The Home Secretary refused the certificate using different criteria than that published.
	Held: Provided the published criteria did not conflict with the Home Secretary's statutory duty, he was under a duty to apply it. He could only renege on the criteria if there was an overriding public interest that he should do so and after he first afforded interested parties a hearing.

A legitimate expectation as a result of a previous course of conduct
Where those exercising public power have done so according to a previous pattern of behaviour which gives rise to a legitimate expectation that they will exercise their power in a similar way in the future, the courts may enforce that legitimate expectation.

Case:	
Council of Civil Service Unions v Minister for the Civil Service [1984] 3 All ER 935	Facts: An Order in Council, enacted under the royal prerogative, gave the Minister for the Civil Service the power to prohibit workers at GCHQ from membership of a union. This was done without consultation with the unions and the Council of Civil Service Unions complained that they had a legitimate expectation of consultation based on past practices.
	Held: The previous course of conduct on behalf of the Government had given rise to a legitimate expectation that the union would always be consulted before changes to employment conditions. However, in the present case, the legitimate expectation was overridden by national security concerns.

Expectation of what?
Two questions arise.

a) Given that it is reasonable for government bodies to change their procedures, what remedy is open to someone who wishes to rely on the old procedure (on the ground that they have a legitimate expectation that it is followed) – are they entitled to rely on the old procedure or simply entitled to make representations to that effect?

b) What may a claimant have a legitimate expectation of – that they will be treated in a particular way (an expectation that a particular procedure will be adopted) or that they are entitled to a particular thing (an expectation of something substantive)?

Case:	
R v North and East Devon Health Authority, ex parte Coughlan [2001] QB 213	Facts: In 1993 the Health Authority moved some severely disabled patients to a new residential home, promising them they could stay there for life. In 1998, the Authority wished to move the patients and close the home.
	Held: Where an authority had made a promise as to how it would behave in the future which gave rise to a substantive, rather than merely procedural, legitimate expectation, it may be so unfair as to amount to an abuse of its power to act contrary to that expectation. The court will balance the public interest in departing from the promise against the importance of the promise to those who relied on it.
	The court discussed three different situations.
	a) Where a promise to act in a particular way is given generally, rather than to an identifiable group of people, the authority should bear in mind its previous policy giving it appropriate weight but no more before deciding to change its course.
	b) If a practice or promise has given rise to a legitimate expectation of consultation or a right to be heard (i.e. a procedural legitimate expectation) induced in particular, identifiable people, it should be departed from only if there is an overriding public interest in doing so.
	c) Where a legitimate expectation has arisen of a substantive benefit, the courts will allow it to be disappointed only if it is fair to do so; factors to be considered here include:
	1) the importance of the expectation to those relying on it;
	2) how many people are relying on it;
	3) the consequences to the authority of honouring the promise.

Checkpoint – Procedural impropriety

Item on checklist:	Done!
I can briefly define the meaning of procedural impropriety.	
I can explain what is required for a consultation to be considered genuine.	
I know the two rules of natural justice.	
I can give an account of the types of things that may be required to ensure the rules of fairness are met.	
I know when apparent bias is likely to automatically invalidate a decision.	
I know the test for bias from the *Porter v Magill* case.	
I can explain what may give rise to a legitimate interest.	
I know the criteria the courts may use when deciding that a substantive, rather than merely procedural, legitimate interest may have arisen.	

Potential exam question

The (fictional) Education Act 2011 gives the Secretary of State for Education the power to remove individual schools from local authority control and to allow them to be run by private organisations for profit. Section 3 of the Act states:

Section 3

1) The Secretary of State for Education alone shall make the decision as to whether a school should be removed from local authority control.

2) The Secretary of State shall take into account the views of those affected by the decision.

3) The Secretary of State may also consult with any parties as he sees fit.

On 10 April 2012, the Secretary of State writes to the headmistress of Muir Hill School informing her that he is considering using his powers under the Education Act 2011 to remove the school from local authority control and to allow it to be run by Shark Ltd, a company specialising in education.

On hearing of this news, Irene Platt, a parent of a child at the school, begins to organise a petition of other parents and teachers against the plans. When informed of this during a radio interview, the Secretary of State says that he will not be swayed by the petition and has no intention of listening to the views of those organising or signing it as they are unlikely to have anything useful to say.

During the same interview, the Secretary of State also announces that the final decision about Muir Hill School will be made by Arthur Brick, a civil servant. On 20 April, Mr Brick writes to the Governors of Muir Hill School asking for their views about whether the school should be removed from local authority control to be run by Shark Ltd. His letter states that he should receive a reply by 25 April and that this should be accompanied by a £25 'processing fee'.

On 30 April, Mr Brick announces that he has decided that Muir Hill School will be removed from local authority control and will be run by Shark Ltd. On the same day, the local newspaper reports that Mr Brick's wife is a major shareholder in Shark Ltd.

Advise the School Governors and Irene Platt about the possible grounds of judicial review that may enable the decision to close the school to be challenged.

Chapter 12

The Convention and the Human Rights Act 1998

In this chapter you will learn:

- the different rights protected by the European Convention on Human Rights;

- the protection of rights in the UK prior to the Human Rights Act 1998;

- the operation of the Human Rights Act 1998;

- vertical and horizontal effect.

12.1 The European Convention on Human Rights: overview

In 1949, following the atrocities committed in the Second World War, the Council of Europe was formed with the intention of restoring civilisation on mainland Europe.

In 1951, the Council produced the European Convention for the Protection of Human Rights and Fundamental Freedoms, more commonly known as the European Convention on Human Rights. The Convention is a treaty; it imposes an obligation on those states that are signatories to it (known as the High Contracting Parties) not to breach certain rights of people within their jurisdictions.

A person who believes their Convention rights have been breached by a signatory state may be able to bring their case before the European Court of Human Rights in Strasbourg.

12.2 The rights

The main Convention rights are contained in Articles 2–12 of the Convention:

Article 2 – right to life.	Article 8 – right to respect for private and family life, home and correspondence.
Article 3 – prohibition of torture and inhuman or degrading treatment.	Article 9 – freedom of thought, conscience and religion.
Article 4 – prohibition of slavery, servitude and forced labour.	Article 10 – freedom of expression.
Article 5 – right to liberty and security of the person.	Article 11 – freedom of assembly and association.
Article 6 – right to a fair trial.	Article 12 – right to marry and found a family.
Article 7 – prohibits retrospective criminal law.	

These rights may be categorised in three different ways: absolute rights, limited rights and qualified rights.

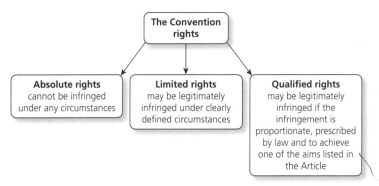

Absolute rights
Absolute rights are those rights that the state is prohibited from infringing under any circumstances. The most obvious example is Article 3:

Article 3 – Prohibition of torture

No one shall be subjected to torture or to inhuman or degrading treatment or punishment.

That is, there are no circumstances in which it is permitted for the state to subject someone to torture or inhuman or degrading treatment.

The other absolute rights are Article 4(1) (no one shall be held in slavery or servitude) and Article 7 (prohibition on retrospective criminal law).

Limited rights

Limited rights are those rights that are limited because they may be legitimately infringed in clearly defined circumstances. For example, the Article 5 right to liberty may be infringed by the lawful arrest and detention of an individual or after their lawful conviction of a crime by a court.

Other limited rights include Article 6 (right to a fair trial) and Article 12 (right to marry).

Qualified rights

Qualified rights may also be infringed but the situations in which this may happen is less clear-cut than with limited rights. Article 8 is an example of a qualified right:

Article 8 – Right to respect for private and family life

1 *Everyone has the right to respect for his private and family life, his home and his correspondence.*
2 *There shall be no interference by a public authority with the exercise of this right except such as is in accordance with the law and is necessary in a democratic society in the interests of national security, public safety or the economic well-being of the country, for the prevention of disorder or crime, for the protection of health or morals, or for the protection of the rights and freedoms of others.*

You will see that this provision is made up of two paragraphs. The first sets out the right in broad terms. The second gives the situations in which that right may be infringed. Yet, for that infringement to be legitimate, certain conditions have to be met:

- the infringement has to be to secure one of the legitimate aims listed in the second paragraph: national security, public safety, etc.;

- the infringement has to be in accordance with the law; i.e. there has to be a legal rule authorising the infringement of the right by the state;

- the infringement has to be necessary in a democratic society; i.e. the infringement has to be proportionate, which means that it should be no more than is necessary to achieve the legitimate aim.

The other qualified rights are:

- Article 9 (freedom of thought, conscience and religion)
- Article 10 (freedom of expression)
- Article 11 (freedom of association and assembly).

Each takes the same format as Article 8: the first paragraph sets out the right and the second sets out the legitimate aims for which it may be infringed so long as the infringement is authorised by law and proportionate.

12.2.1 Article 1, Article 13 and Article 14

Article 1 – Obligation to respect human rights

The High Contracting Parties shall secure to everyone within their jurisdiction the rights and freedoms defined in Section I of this Convention.

Article 1 of the Convention simply obliges the signatory states to ensure that the Convention rights of everyone in their jurisdiction are protected.

Article 13 – Right to an effective remedy

Everyone whose rights and freedoms as set forth in this Convention are violated shall have an effective remedy before a national authority notwithstanding that the violation has been committed by persons acting in an official capacity.

Article 13 obliges the signatory states to ensure that those whose Convention rights are infringed have a remedy before a national authority.

Article 14 – Prohibition of discrimination

The enjoyment of the rights and freedoms set forth in this Convention shall be secured without discrimination on any ground such as sex, race, colour, language, religion, political or other opinion, national or social origin, association with a national minority, property, birth or other status.

Article 14 is not a prohibition on discrimination in general but, rather, it prohibits discrimination with regard to the Convention rights. So, you cannot simply claim that you have been discriminated against to successfully claim a breach of Article 14; you have to demonstrate that you have been discriminated against with regard to the subject matter of one of the Convention rights.

However, you do not have to demonstrate an infringement of one of the substantive rights to succeed in a claim under Article 14; you merely have to demonstrate that you have been discriminated against with regard to the subject matter of a substantive right.

Case:	
Regina (Hindawi and Another) v Secretary of State for the Home Department [2006] UKHL 54	Facts: The Criminal Justice Act 1991 gave the Home Secretary the discretion as to whether prisoners who might be deported on release (and so were non-UK nationals) could be granted early release. For UK nationals, the issue of early release was considered by the parole board. The Home Secretary rejected the claimants' applications for early release and they argued that this breached their Article 5 right to liberty and Article 14 right not to be subject to discrimination in the provision of the Convention rights.
	Held: There was no breach of Article 5: they had been lawfully detained and had no right of early release under the Convention. However, the court granted a declaration that the relevant sections of the Criminal Justice Act were incompatible with Article 14 because they provided for differential treatment of prisoners on the grounds of nationality.
	Lord Bingham: *'The prohibition of discrimination in Article 14 thus extends beyond the enjoyment of the rights and freedoms which the Convention and Protocols require each State to guarantee. It applies also to those additional rights, falling within the general scope of any Convention article, for which the State has voluntarily decided to provide.'*

Case:	
Stec v United Kingdom **[2005] 41 EHRR SE 295**	*'The Court recalls that Article 14 complements the other substantive provisions of the Convention and the Protocols. It has no independent existence since it has effect solely in relation to "the enjoyment of the rights and freedoms" safeguarded by those provisions ... The application of Article 14 does not necessarily presuppose the violation of one of the substantive rights guaranteed by the Convention. It is necessary but it is also sufficient for the facts of the case to fall "within the ambit" of one or more of the Convention Articles.'*

12.2.2 The protocols

Other rights are contained in the protocols to the Convention. These are additional agreements among the High Contracting Parties, though a signatory state may choose not to become a party to a particular protocol.

I wish to note the following four protocol rights because they also have effect in UK law by virtue of the Human Rights Act 1998 (HRA):

- Protocol 1, Article 1 which guarantees the right of peaceful enjoyment of one's property;

- Protocol 1, Article 2 which guarantees a right of education and a respect for that education to be in conformity with the parents' religious or philosophical wishes;

- Protocol 1, Article 3 guarantees free elections;

- Protocol 13 abolishes the death penalty.

12.2.3 Reservations and derogations

A reservation allows states to exempt themselves from certain parts of a treaty to which they are signatories. A reservation can be made only at the time of ratification.

A derogation allows a signatory state to suspend some of their obligations under a treaty. With regard to the European Convention on Human Rights, such derogations are permitted by Article 15. The following should be noted:

- The signatory states may only derogate from the Convention in time of war or other public emergency threatening the life of the nation, but only so far as is required by the situation.

- There can be no derogation from:
  - Article 2 (the right to life) except in the case of deaths resulting from lawful acts of war;
  - Article 3 (the prohibition of torture, inhuman or degrading treatment or imprisonment);
  - Article 4, paragraph 1 (the prohibition of slavery or servitude);
  - Article 7 (prohibition on retrospective law).

12.2.4 Margin of appreciation

The European Court has developed the doctrine of permitting the signatory states a margin of appreciation when deciding how they may best meet their obligations under the Convention. Briefly put, this doctrine recognises that different states may protect the rights of their citizens in different ways, and in ways that differ from how the European Court of Human Rights would have protected the rights. It therefore allows each state an area of discretion as to how it may best protect the rights contained in the Convention.

12.3 The European Court of Human Rights

Those who believe that their Convention rights have been breached by one of the signatory states may be able to bring their case before the European Court of Human Rights in Strasbourg.

The Court is made up of one judge from each signatory state. When an application is made to the court, three judges assess its admissibility.

The admissibility criteria, which one must satisfy in order to bring a case before the court, are given in Article 35 of the Convention:

- the applicant must have exhausted all domestic remedies;

- the application must be made within six months of the date of the final decision;

- the applicant must not be anonymous;

- the application must raise a matter that is not substantially the same as a matter that has already been ruled on by the Court;

- the application must be compatible with the provisions of the Convention and must not be manifestly ill-founded or an abuse of the right of application.

If an application is admissible, and the parties cannot come to a friendly settlement, the case may go to the Court. The Court usually sits as a chamber of seven judges. In important cases, the Court may sit as a Grand Chamber of 17 judges. The Grand Chamber may also hear appeals against judgments by an ordinary chamber.

If the signatory state is found to have breached the Convention rights, the courts may order it to pay damages and reimburse legal costs. Where necessary, the signatory state is also obliged to address the matter and alter its law to bring it into line with the Convention.

12.4 Protection of rights in the UK before the HRA

Traditionally, citizens in the UK have the right to do everything that the law does not prohibit. So, for instance, you have the right to walk down the street smoking a cigarette because there is no law that forbids it. Such rights are sometimes referred to as negative rights: you can engage in the activity because it is not prohibited by law. They may be contrasted with positive rights, such as the Convention rights, which exist because they are positively guaranteed by some enactment.

Case:	
***Malone v Metropolitan Police Commissioner* [1979] Ch 344**	Facts: Malone complained that a listening device placed by the police on his telephone line, on the premises of his telephone provider, was unlawful.
	Held: There was no law preventing the police intercepting his phone conversations in this way and so it was lawful.
	Megarry VC: *'England, it may be said, is not a country where everything is forbidden except what is expressly permitted: it is a country where everything is permitted except what is expressly forbidden.'*

12.4.1 Protection of the Convention rights in the UK prior to the HRA

While the UK was one of the original signatories of the Convention in the 1950s, the Convention rights did not become part of UK law until the coming into force of the HRA on 2 October 2000.

> Note: While the HRA was enacted in 1998, it did not come into force until 2 October 2000.
>
> This meant that a UK citizen who believed their rights had been infringed had no direct cause of action in the UK courts; rather, they could only bring their case before the (now defunct) European Commission of Human Rights and then the European Court of Human Rights.
>
> Prior to the HRA, the UK courts would only take the Convention into account if the law was ambiguous in order to resolve that ambiguity.

Cases:	
Reg. v Chief Immigration Officer, Heathrow Airport, Ex parte Salamat Bibi [1976] 1 WLR 979	Lord Denning MR: *'The position as I understand it is that if there is any ambiguity in our statutes, or uncertainty in our law, then these courts can look to the Convention as an aid to clear up the ambiguity and uncertainty ... But I would dispute altogether that the Convention is part of our law. Treaties and declarations do not become part of our law until they are made law by Parliament.'*
R v Secretary of State for the Home Department, ex parte Brind and others [1991] 1 AC 696	Lord Bridge: *'[L]ike any other treaty obligations which have not been embodied in the law by statute, the Convention is not part of the domestic law, [and] the courts accordingly have no power to enforce Convention rights directly [so], if domestic legislation conflicts with the Convention, the courts must nevertheless enforce it. But it is already well settled that, in construing any provision in domestic legislation which is ambiguous in the sense that it is capable of a meaning which either conforms to or conflicts with the Convention, the courts will presume that Parliament intended to legislate in conformity with the Convention, not in conflict with it.'*

Checkpoint – The European Convention on Human Rights

Item on checklist:	Done!
I can define the different categories of rights protected by the Convention: absolute rights, limited rights and qualified rights.	
I can explain how Article 14 operates.	
I know the criteria that must exist before a state may derogate from its obligations under the Convention.	
I can explain the doctrine of the margin of appreciation.	
I can explain the concept of negative rights and distinguish them from positive rights.	
I can explain the protection given to the Convention rights in the UK prior to the HRA.	

12.5 The Human Rights Act 1998

The HRA attempts to make the Convention rights an integral part of UK law. The Act obliges public authorities not to act in a way that is incompatible with the Convention rights. It also imposes certain duties on the UK courts:

- It obliges them to take into account judgments and decisions of the European Court of Human Rights, and other Convention bodies, when deciding a matter that involves a Convention right.

- It requires the courts to try to interpret legislation so that it conforms with the Convention rights.

- If the courts cannot interpret legislation in this way, the higher courts may make a declaration that the legislation in question is incompatible with the Convention rights.

If a declaration of incompatibility has been made, the Act allows a government minister to use secondary legislation to alter primary legislation so as to make it compatible.

The Convention rights to which the Act gives effect are contained in Schedule 1 of the HRA. They are:

- Articles 2–12 and Article 14 of the Convention (see Section 12.2, above);

- Articles 1, 2 and 3 of Protocol 1 and Protocol 13 (see Section 12.2.2, above).

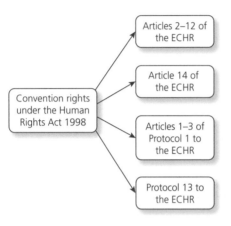

12.5.1 Significant provisions of the HRA

12.5.1.1 Section 2: Interpretation of Convention rights

Section 2 of the Act obliges the UK courts to take into account judgments and decisions of the European Court of Human Rights, and other Convention bodies (some of which are now defunct), when deciding a matter that involves a Convention right.

12.5.1.2 Sections 3, 4 and 10 of the HRA

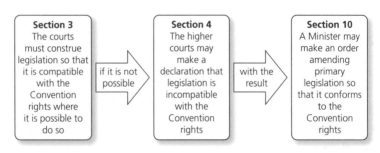

It is useful to look at ss 3, 4 and 10 of the Act together because they apply to legislation that is not, on the face of it, compatible with the Convention rights.

Section 3

Section 3 – Interpretation of Legislation

1) So far as it is possible to do so, primary legislation and subordinate legislation must be read and given effect in a way which is compatible with the Convention rights.

2) This section–
   a) applies to primary legislation and subordinate legislation whenever enacted;
   b) does not affect the validity, continuing operation or enforcement of any incompatible primary legislation; and
   c) does not affect the validity, continuing operation or enforcement of any incompatible subordinate legislation if (disregarding any possibility of revocation) primary legislation prevents removal of the incompatibility.

Section 3 of the HRA instructs the courts to interpret legislation in such a way that it conforms with the Convention rights. There are three important things to note about this provision.

a) It applies to legislation 'whenever enacted'. This means that it applies to legislation enacted both before and after the HRA.

b) If legislation cannot be interpreted so as to conform to the Convention rights, this does not affect the validity of
   1) primary legislation or
   2) secondary legislation where primary legislation prevents the courts removing the incompatibility.

c) The courts may only interpret legislation to conform to the Convention rights 'so far as it is possible to do so'.

This last point is important. It is a reminder that while the courts must try to construe legislation to conform to the Convention rights, they are not legislators. However, s 3 leaves the position less than clear; should the courts refuse to give legislation a meaning that linguistically or grammatically the words cannot bear or should they be prepared to ascribe a meaning that is different than one that could naturally be given to the words used?

The following two cases give some indication of the approaches being adopted by the courts.

Case:

R v A [2002] 1 AC 45	Facts: Section 41 of the Youth Justice and Criminal Evidence Act 1999 restricted the right of a defendant in a rape trial from raising evidence, and questioning the complainant, about her sexual history. The defendant in this case argued that this was a breach of his Article 6 right to a fair trial. The question for the court was whether s 41 should be interpreted so as to comply with Article 6.
	Held: Section 41 should be construed in the light of Article 6 but what was permissible in each case was a question for the trial judge who should bear in mind the need to protect a complainant from indignity and humiliating questions.
	The following speeches from the case seem to illustrate slightly different approaches: Lord Hope seems to advocate a more cautious approach than Lord Steyn.
	Lord Steyn: *'the interpretative obligation under section 3 of the 1998 Act is a strong one ... [I]t will sometimes be necessary to adopt an interpretation which linguistically may appear strained. The techniques to be used will not only involve the reading down of express language in a statute but also the implication of provisions.'*
	Lord Hope: *'The rule of construction which section 3 lays down is quite unlike any previous rule of statutory interpretation ... But the rule is only a rule of interpretation. It does not entitle the judges to act as legislators.'*

Case:	
***Ghaidan v Godin-Memdoza* [2004] UKHL 30**	Facts: The claimant landlord wanted to evict the defendant tenant from his property. The defendant had lived at the property with his partner, the original tenant, in a same-sex relationship for 18 years. The question for the court was whether the defendant was a statutory tenant under the Rent Act 1977. A statutory tenant was the spouse of the original tenant, which included living with the original tenant as their husband or wife. At issue was whether the court could interpret the Rent Act protection given to couples living as husband and wife to couples in same-sex relationships. If it could not, then there may be a breach of Article 14, which prohibits discrimination with regard to the Convention rights, in this case the Article 8 right of respect for one's home. This is because a same-sex partner would be treated differently than the partner in a heterosexual relationship.
	Held: (By a majority) The Rent Act 1977 should be construed as giving statutory tenant status to the partner of a stable same-sex couple. Section 3 of the HRA may require a court to give a meaning to legislation other than that which it would normally have, and perhaps contrary to what Parliament intended. However, s 3 does not permit the courts to go against the general, underlying rationale of the legislation.

Workpoint

What approach do you think the courts should take when attempting to interpret legislation in a way that is compatible with the Convention rights? Should they attempt to remain true to the legislation as enacted by Parliament and not go beyond the natural meaning of the words or should they go beyond the natural meaning so as to maintain compatibility with the Convention rights? What are the reasons for your answer?

Section 4

Under s 4, if the higher courts are satisfied that primary legislation is not compatible with the Convention rights, they may make a declaration of incompatibility. The higher courts are:

• the Supreme Court

• the Judicial Committee of the Privy Council

• the Courts-Martial Appeal Court

• the High Court of Justiciary or the Court of Session (Scotland)

• the High Court or the Court of Appeal (England, Wales and Northern Ireland).

Importantly, a declaration of incompatibility does not affect the continuing validity of the legislation in question.

Workpoint

Why do you think Parliament decided that neither a failure to interpret legislation to conform to the Convention right nor a declaration of incompatibility should affect the validity of the legislation in question?

Section 10

Under s 10, a minister may make an order amending primary legislation to bring it in line with the Convention rights if:

• a declaration of incompatibility has been made under s 4 or

• a decision of the European Court of Human Rights has made it clear that a provision of UK legislation is not compatible with the Convention rights.

Section 10 therefore gives a minister an extraordinary power: to use secondary legislation to alter primary legislation. A provision such as this is sometimes referred to as a Henry VIII (Henry the Eighth) clause.

Definition

Henry VIII clause: A provision in one Act of Parliament that gives ministers the power to alter other Acts of Parliament.

Do you think the power given to ministers under s 10 of the HRA is compatible with parliamentary sovereignty (see Chapter 6)?

12.5.1.3 Statement of compatibility

Section 19 of the HRA requires a minister in charge of a Bill going through Parliament to make a written statement before second reading in either House of Parliament that, in his or her opinion,

- the legislation is compatible with the Convention rights or

- the legislation is not compatible with the Convention rights but the Government wishes to proceed with it anyway.

What if no such statement is made? Do you think the courts would be prepared to rule the legislation invalid because the procedure set out in s 19 has not been followed (see Section 6.5.1)?

12.5.2 Section 6 and public authorities

Section 6 is one of the most significant provisions of the HRA.

Section 6(1) states that it is unlawful for a public authority to act in a way that is incompatible with the Convention rights. However, under s 6(2) a public authority does not act unlawfully if it is prevented by primary legislation from acting compatibly with the Convention rights.

Section 6 – Acts of Public Authorities

1) It is unlawful for a public authority to act in a way which is incompatible with a Convention right.

2) Subsection (1) does not apply to an act if–

   a) as the result of one or more provisions of primary legislation, the authority could not have acted differently; or

   b) in the case of one or more provisions of, or made under, primary legislation which cannot be read or given effect in a way which is compatible with the Convention rights, the authority was acting so as to give effect to or enforce those provisions.

The question arises as to what amounts to a public authority. The Act does not give a definitive answer to this question but it is clear there two categories of public authority.

a) Core or pure public authorities – these are bodies that are obviously part of the state. They include central governmental bodies, local governmental bodies, the police, the prison service and the courts themselves. Such bodies must act in conformity with the Convention rights in all that they do.

b) Functional public authorities (also known as section 6(3)(b) public authorities or hybrid public authorities) – s 6(3)(b) of the Act states that public authorities include any body that exercises functions of a public nature. Such bodies must act in conformity with the Convention rights with regard to those functions but not with regard to private acts.

Section 6

3) In this section 'public authority' includes–
    a) a court or tribunal, and
    b) any person certain of whose functions are functions of a public nature

    . . .

5) In relation to a particular act, a person is not a public authority by virtue only of subsection (3)(b) if the nature of the act is private.

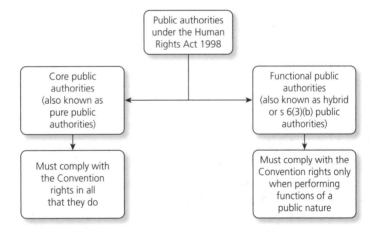

Functions of a public nature

Often it will be obvious whether a particular function is one of a public nature. Elliott and Thomas give the following example:

'If a local authority (a core public authority) contracts out the cleaning of its offices to a company, the HRA will not apply: cleaning offices – even those of a core public authority – is not a public function. Equally obviously, if the Prison Service contracts out the running of a prison to a company, many of the functions performed by the latter will be public in nature, bearing in mind that it will, through its employees, be exercising the coercive powers of the state.'

(Elliott, M. and Thomas, R., *Public Law*, 2011, Oxford: Oxford University Press)

Similarly, the leading case *Aston Cantlow* gives relatively clear guidance.

Case:	
***Aston Cantlow and Wilmcote with Billesley Parochial Church Council v Wallbank* [2003] UKHL 37**	Facts: The owners of a property were liable to pay for repairs to the chancel of a neighbouring church. They argued that the church council were infringing their property rights under the Convention by attempting to enforce payment for repairs. A preliminary question for the court was whether the church council were exercising a function of a public nature when attempting to enforce payment.
	Held: The council were not exercising a function of a public nature; they were attempting to enforce a civil debt which was not analogous to the duties performed by the state. The court stated that relevant factors when assessing whether a function is of a public nature are: • whether the body is exercising powers derived from statute; • whether it is publicly funded; • whether it is taking the place of local or central government; or • whether it is providing a public service.

However, other cases have caused some confusion. In the *Donoghue* case, the Court of Appeal appeared to examine the nature of the body and its relationship with a pure public authority rather than the nature of the function undertaken.

Case:	
***Poplar Housing and Regeneration Community Association Ltd v Donoghue* [2001] EWCA Civ 595**	Facts: Donoghue was homeless. The local authority had a statutory duty to provide accommodation for the homeless but not for those who were intentionally homeless. The authority provided accommodation for Donoghue pending a decision as to whether she was intentionally homeless. In the meantime, it transferred some of its housing to the Poplar Housing and Regeneration Community Association, including the property in which Donoghue had been accommodated. It was decided that Donoghue was intentionally homeless and the Association sought possession of the property. She claimed that evicting her would be an infringement of her Article 8 right to respect for her family and home. A preliminary question was whether the Association was exercising a function of a public nature when providing accommodation to Donoghue.
	Held: The Association was exercising a function of a public nature but the eviction of Donoghue did not infringe her Article 8 rights.
	Two factors seemed to be relevant in the Court's decision that the Association was exercising a function of a public nature.
	a) Donoghue was originally a tenant of the local authority (a core public authority under the HRA) and it was intended that she should not have a different level of protection of her Convention rights when the property was transferred to the Association.
	b) The Association had been created by the local authority, five members of the local authority sat on the Board of the Association and the Association was subject to the local authority's control. This created a close relationship between the local authority and the Association, which was indicative that the activities of the latter amounted to functions of a public nature.

In the following two cases, the courts seemed to reach conclusions that are contrary to the rationale underlying s 6(3)(b).

Cases:	
R (Heather) v Leonard Cheshire Foundation [2002] EWCA Civ 366	Facts: Surrey County Council was under a statutory duty to provide residential care for Heather. The Council contracted with a private organisation, the Leonard Cheshire Foundation, to provide this care on its behalf. The Foundation decided to close the care home where Heather resided. Heather challenged this as a breach of her Article 8 rights and the issue before the court was whether the Foundation was exercising a function of a public nature when providing the care.
	Held: The Foundation was not exercising a function of a public nature.
	Lord Woolf: *'If the authority itself provides accommodation, it is providing a public function. It is also providing a public function if it makes arrangements for the accommodation to be provided by LCF. However, if a body which is a charity, like LCF, provides accommodation to those to whom the authority owes a duty … it does not follow that the charity is performing a public function.'*
YL v Birmingham City Council [2007] UKHL 27	Facts: Birmingham City Council was under a statutory duty to provide residential care for YL. It contracted with a third party, Southern Cross Health Care, to provide this care on its behalf. Southern Cross sought to terminate YL's right to remain in the home and she argued that this amounted to a breach of her Article 8 right to respect for her family and home life. The question of whether Southern Cross was exercising a function of a public nature with regard to YL was tried as a preliminary matter.
	Held: (By a majority of 3 to 2) Southern Cross was not exercising a function of a public nature when providing residential care for YL.

In both the *Heather* and *YL* cases, the claimants would have had the protection of the Convention rights if their care had been provided by the Councils themselves. It is not easy to understand how the courts could decide that a function that the Councils were under a statutory duty to facilitate was not a function of a public nature if performed by a third party under a contract with the Council. This point has been made by Paul Craig:

'It is difficult to see why the nature of a function should alter if it is contracted out, rather than being performed in house. If it is a public function when undertaken in house, it should be equally so when contracted out.'

(Craig, P.P. 'Contracting Out, the Human Rights Act and the Scope of Judicial Review' (2002) 118 LQR 551, 556)

Moreover, s 6(3)(b) seemed to be designed to cover this very situation:

• where a government body contracts with a private organisation to provide functions which the government body is under a public duty to provide the intention was surely that those to whom the function is delivered are not thereby removed from the protection of the HRA.

Indeed, Parliament has now made it clear that when private bodies are exercising the kind of function performed in the *Heather* and *YL* cases they are exercising functions of a public nature under the HRA.
    Section 145(1) of the Health and Social Care Act 2008:

(1) A person ('P') who provides accommodation, together with nursing or personal care, in a care home for an individual under arrangements made with P under the relevant statutory provisions is to be taken for the purposes of subsection (3)(b) of section 6 of the Human Rights Act 1998 (c. 42) (acts of public authorities) to be exercising a function of a public nature in doing so.

However, this only clarifies one type of function: the provision of accommodation along with nursing or personal care. The reasoning of the majority of the House of Lords in the *YL* case is still binding on other types of function. This means that bodies not performing this kind of nursing/accommodation activity but otherwise exercising functions that a public body is under a duty to exercise may still not be found to be exercising functions of a public nature.

12.5.2.1 Vertical and horizontal effect of the HRA

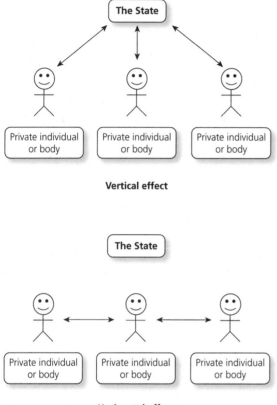

Vertical effect

Horizontal effect

If a law has horizontal effect, it affects the legal relationship between private individuals or bodies. If a law has vertical effect, it affects the legal relationship between the private individual or bodies and the state.

We have seen that under s 6 of the HRA it is unlawful for public authorities (i.e. government bodies or those exercising governmental power) to act incompatibly with the Convention rights. In this way, the Act has vertical effect: it governs the relationship between the citizen and the state.

There is no corresponding obligation placed on private bodies (other than those exercising functions of a public nature under s 6(3)(b)). You cannot, therefore, bring a case to court on the ground that a private individual or organisation has infringed your Convention rights.

However, s 6(3)(a) of the Act states that courts and tribunals are themselves public authorities.

Section 6
3) In this section 'public authority' includes–
*   a) a court or tribunal.*

This means that courts and tribunals are obliged to act compatibly with the Convention rights in all that they do, including the way they decide cases. The consequence of this is that, while a citizen cannot bring a case to court on the ground that a private body has infringed their Convention rights, if they can bring a case on some other cause of action, the court must take into account the Convention rights of both parties when deciding the case.

For instance, imagine you had a neighbour who played extremely loud music throughout the night so that your sleep was constantly disturbed. While this would damage your home and family life, you could not bring legal action against your neighbour for breaching your Article 8 rights because your neighbour is not a public authority. You may, however, bring an action for statutory nuisance under s 82 of the Environmental Protection Act 1990 and, in hearing your case, the court would have to take into account your Article 8 rights.

It is in this way that the HRA has indirect horizontal effect:

• horizontal because it can affect relations between private bodies;

• indirect because individuals cannot apply to the courts claiming that a private body has infringed their Convention rights but if they bring another case, the court must decide that case in accordance with the Convention rights.

Case:	
***Campbell v MGN Ltd* [2004] 2 AC 457**	Baroness Hale: *'The 1998 Act does not create any new cause of action between private persons. But if there is a relevant cause of action applicable, the court as a public authority must act compatibly with both parties' Convention rights.'*

Checkpoint – The Human Rights Act 1998

Item on checklist:	Done!
I know the rights to which the HRA gives effect (known as the Convention rights in the Act).	
I can explain the obligation imposed on courts by s 2 of the HRA.	
I can explain how ss 3, 4 and 10 function and how they may be thought of as operating together with regard to legislation.	
I know the obligation placed on ministers by s 19 of the HRA.	
I can distinguish between core public authorities and functional public authorities.	
I can explain why the meaning of 'functions of a public nature' is unclear following decisions of the courts.	
I can explain why the HRA may have indirect horizontal effect.	

Potential exam question

Explain the relationship between ss 3, 4 and 10 of the Human Rights Act 1998. Also, explain the meaning of 'public authority' under the Act.

Chapter 13

Freedom of expression

In this chapter you will learn:

- the protection given to freedom of expression by the European Convention on Human Rights;

- the importance of a free press;

- contempt of court under the Contempt of Court Act 1981;

- the protection given to jounalists' sources in UK law and under the European Convention on Human Rights.

13.1 Article 10 and freedom of expression

Freedom of expression is protected by Article 10 of the European Convention on Human Rights.

Article 10 Freedom of expression
1   *Everyone has the right to freedom of expression. This right shall include freedom to hold opinions and to receive and impart information and ideas without interference by public authority and regardless of frontiers. This Article shall not prevent States from requiring the licensing of broadcasting, television or cinema enterprises.*
2   *The exercise of these freedoms, since it carries with it duties and responsibilities, may be subject to such formalities, conditions, restrictions or penalties as are prescribed by law and are necessary in a democratic society, in the interests of national security, territorial integrity or public safety, for the prevention of disorder or crime, for the protection of health or morals, for the protection of the reputation or rights of others, for preventing the disclosure of information received in confidence, or for maintaining the authority and impartiality of the judiciary.*

Article 10 is a qualified right (see Section 12.2). This means that the right, set out in the first paragraph of the Article, may be lawfully infringed as long as the infringement is:

- prescribed by law;

- to secure one of the legitimate aims listed in the second paragraph of the Article;

- necessary in a democratic society (i.e. is proportionate).

The European Court of Human Rights explained the meaning and importance of freedom of expression in the *Handyside* case:

Case:	
***Handyside v United Kingdom* (1976) 1 EHRR 737**	*'Freedom of expression constitutes one of the essential foundations of [democratic] society, one of the basic conditions for its progress and for the development of every man.... [I]t is applicable not only to "information" or "ideas" that are favourably received or regarded as inoffensive or as a matter of indifference, but also to those that offend, shock or disturb the State or any sector of the population. Such are the demands of that pluralism, tolerance and broadmindedness without which there is no "democratic society".'*

We can see, then, that the Court considers freedom of expression to be an essential foundation of society.

We can also see that the Court considers the values of *'pluralism, tolerance and broadmindedness'* to be vital for a democratic society. This means that freedom of expression exists to protect information that may *'offend, shock or disturb'*; it does not simply protect speech, information or ideas that are inoffensive.

Workpoint

It could be argued that the protection of the offensive, shocking and disturbing are central to freedom of expression because the protection of the inoffensive is not necessary. Explain this argument and try to develop some counter-arguments.

It is worth noting here that s 12 of the Human Rights Act 1998 gives particular attention to freedom of expression. It obliges the courts not to grant an injunction to prevent the publication of material unless:

- the applicant has taken all practicable steps to notify the respondent (i.e. those affected by the injunction), or

- there are compelling reasons not to notify the respondent.

Also, when considering whether to grant an injunction, s 12 obliges the courts to have particular regard to the Convention right of freedom of expression where the material concerned appears to have some artistic, literary or journalistic merit.

Checkpoint – freedom of expression	
Item on checklist:	**Done!**
I can explain why freedom of expression is considered important.	
I can explain when it might be considered lawful for the right of freedom of expression to be infringed under Article 10.	

13.2 Contempt of court and freedom of the press in the UK

Freedom of expression may be lawfully restricted in a number of ways in the UK including:

- the law relating to obscenity;

- common law offences such as:
  - conspiracy to corrupt public morals (see *Shaw v DPP* [1962] AC 220)
  - conspiracy to outrage public decency (see *Knuller v DPP* [1973] AC 435 and *R v Gibson* [1990] 2 QB 619);

- offences under the Racial and Religious Hatred Act 2006 such as using threatening words and behaviour; displaying, distributing or publishing threatening material;

- offences under the Official Secrets Acts;

- increasingly, offences relating to terrorism;

- offences amounting to an improper use of a public electronic communications network (including email and social networking sites) under the Communications Act 2003.

However, I want to focus on the law of contempt of court, particularly as it attempts to regulate the press. This is because, in this area of law, we see two important considerations being balanced against each other:

- freedom of the press and

- the interests of justice.

13.2.1 Freedom of the press

A free press is considered important because it is one of the main ways by which governments may be held to account and, consequently, is a significant guarantor of a healthy, functioning democracy. Often it is the press – and the work of individual or teams of investigative journalists – who shine a light into the darkest corners of government activity. This is particularly the case in the UK where Parliament, whose formal role includes holding the executive to account, often takes a subservient, supine role in the face of a dominant Government.

> ### Workpoint
>
> Identify as many current or recent political scandals as you can where the press has played a significant role in bringing the matter to public attention and thereby holding those in power to account.

However, the absolute freedom of the press is restricted in a number of ways, including by the law of contempt of court.

The law of contempt of court seeks to balance the right of freedom of expression against other values such as the right to a fair trail, the need to safeguard the administration of justice and the need to maintain the dignity of the court.

There are two areas that I wish to examine:

- publications prejudicial to the course of justice;

- the protection of journalistic sources.

13.2.2 Publications prejudicial to the course of justice

This area of law attempts to ensure that the likelihood of a fair trial in either civil or criminal proceedings is not harmed by publications that may create a risk that a trial is prejudiced or impeded.

The law here is governed by the Contempt of Court Act 1981. Under ss 1 and 2 of the Act, it is a contempt of court if a publication creates a substantial risk that the course of justice in legal proceedings will be seriously impeded or prejudiced.

The offence is committed regardless of whether the substantial risk to the course of justice was intended by those responsible for the publication.

However, the offence may only be committed once the proceedings in question are 'active'. The meaning of 'active' is given in Schedule 1 of the Act.

* For criminal proceedings, a case becomes active when:
  * there is an arrest without warrant;
  * a warrant is issued for an arrest;
  * a summons is issued;
  * an individual is charged, orally, with an offence.

  The proceedings remain active until there is an acquittal, sentence or discontinuance of the proceedings.

* In civil cases, the proceedings become active when the case is set down for trial (listed to be heard in a particular term) or when a date for the trial or hearing is fixed. They remain active until the proceedings are disposed of, discontinued or withdrawn.

The operation of ss 1 and 2 of the Contempt of Court Act 1981 can be seen in the following case, which concerned newspaper reports following the murder of Joanna Yates in 2010.

Case:	
***Attorney General v MGN Ltd and another* [2012] 1 WLR 2408**	Facts: Christopher Jefferies was arrested on suspicion of the murder of Joanna Yates. He was later released without charge and is, in fact, wholly innocent of the offence. Another man was subsequently convicted of the murder. During the period of Mr Jefferies' arrest some national newspapers published articles alleging a number of things about Mr

Jefferies including that he was a 'peeping Tom', that he had a friendship with a convicted paedophile and linking him to another murder committed 30 years previously. The Attorney General applied to the court to find the papers in question in contempt of court under ss 1 and 2 of the Contempt of Court Act 1981 on the ground that their reporting created a substantial risk that the course of justice in proceedings would be seriously impeded or prejudiced.

Held: The vilification of Mr Jefferies in the newspaper articles published during the time of his arrest created a substantial risk of prejudicing any possible proceedings. The risk was created even though, in the event, Mr Jefferies did not stand trial for any offence. Moreover, the articles may have also deterred or discouraged witnesses coming forward and providing information that might have been useful to Mr Jefferies. For this reason they also created a risk of impediment to the course of justice.

13.2.2.1 Defences

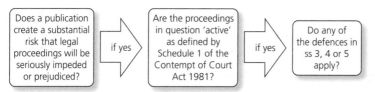

There are three defences to the offence created by ss 1 and 2 of the Contempt of Court Act 1981. Respectively, these are contained in ss 3, 4 and 5 of the Act.

Defences to the offence created by ss 1 and 2 of the Contempt of Court Act 1981	
Section 3 Defence of innocent publication or distribution	Under s 3, a person will not be guilty of contempt of court if they did not know and had no reason to suspect that the proceedings in question are active as long as they have taken all reasonable care.
Section 4 Contemporary reports of proceedings	Under s 4, a person is not guilty of contempt of court if they publish a fair and accurate report of proceedings held in public, as long as the report is contemporaneous and published in good faith.

Section 5 Discussion of public affairs	Under s 5, a person will not be guilty of contempt of court if the publication makes or is part of a discussion in *'good faith of public affairs or other matters of general public interest'* and where the *'risk of impediment or prejudice to particular legal proceedings is merely incidental to the discussion'*.

The section 5 defence can be seen in the case of *Attorney General v English*.

Case:	
***Attorney General v English* [1983] 1 AC 116**	Facts: A national newspaper published an article supporting a parliamentary candidate, Marilyn Carr, whose election campaign argued against an alleged practice whereby new-born disabled babies were left to die. The article was published on the third day of the murder trial of a paediatrician who was accused of allowing a Down's syndrome baby to die of starvation. The issue was whether the article amounted to a contempt of court under the Contempt of Court Act 1981 by causing a substantial risk that the course of justice in the trial would be seriously prejudiced.
	Held: The article did not amount to a contempt of court; while it was capable of prejudicing the jury it was a discussion in good faith of a matter of public interest and the risk of prejudice was incidental to that discussion.
	Lord Diplock stated of the decision: *'To hold otherwise would have prevented Mrs Carr from putting forward and obtaining publicity for what was a main plank in her election programme and would have stifled all discussion in the press upon the wider controversy about mercy killing [during the period of the murder trial].'*

The following case of *Attorney-General v Random House Group Ltd* is interesting because it discusses aspects of the offence under the Contempt of Court Act 1981, particularly the difference between a risk of serious prejudice and a risk of serious impediment to legal proceedings. It also considers the section 5 defence of whether the risk to proceedings is merely incidental to a discussion that a publication makes or forms part. The case also considers the issue of proportionality.

Case:	
Attorney-General v Random House Group Ltd [2009] EWHC 1727	Facts: A passage in a book written by a former Assistant Commissioner of the Metropolitan Police described an investigation into a plot to blow up an aircraft. At the subsequent trial of those suspected of this plot, the jury failed to reach a verdict against three of the defendants on one of the charges and against four defendants on all the charges. A retrial was therefore ordered. The book was published before the end of the retrial and about 800 copies of it were sold. An interim injunction was granted to prevent further sales of the book and the question for the court in the present case was whether that injunction should be extended until the trial had concluded.

Held: The injunction should be continued. The court found:

- while there was a risk that a juror who read the book might be prejudiced, this risk was remote;
- there was a risk that the trial might be seriously impeded if the book was allowed to go back on sale. This was because the defence team might make applications to discharge the jury after making applications to discern whether any of the jurors had read the book. There was, then, a risk that the judge would discharge the jury or that, if he did not, this would be a ground for an appeal;
- regarding the defence in s 5, the court held that the book could be considered to be a discussion of public affairs and of general public interest. However, because it gave a description of the facts that led to the criminal prosecution, it could not be said that the risk of impediment to proceedings was merely incidental to the discussion in the book;
- the court considered whether a continuing injunction was necessary and proportionate and held that the significant financial cost to the publisher was outweighed by the financial cost if the trial was impeded. In addition, it was of the highest importance that the trial should not be seriously impeded and that it should be fair.

Checkpoint – Publications prejudicial to the course of justice	
Item on checklist:	**Done!**
I know the ingredients of contempt of court under ss 1 and 2 of the Contempt of Court Act 1981.	
I can explain what is meant by the word 'active' as it is used here.	
I can explain the defence under s 3 of the Contempt of Court Act 1981.	
I can explain the defence under s 4 of the Contempt of Court Act 1981.	
I can explain the defence under s 5 of the Contempt of Court Act 1981.	

13.2.3 The protection of journalists' sources

It will often be the case that a piece of journalism has been informed by the use of a source – a person who has passed information to the journalist author of that piece. In such cases, the target of the journalism – who may be a company or government department – may want to identify the person who has leaked the information to the press so as to take disciplinary action against them. However, the ability of the press to hold those in power to account, which is the main rationale for a free press, means that such sources should be protected. Without such protection those who would otherwise provide information to the press about wrongdoings may be discouraged from doing so.

The importance of protecting journalistic sources from disclosure was recognised by Lord Salmon in the *British Steel Corporation v Granada Television* case and by the European Court of Human Rights in the *Goodwin* case.

Case:	
***British Steel Corporation v Granada Television Ltd* [1981] AC 1096**	Lord Salmon: *'The freedom of the press depends on [the immunity of journalists' sources]. Were it to disappear, so would the sources from which its information is obtained; and the public would be deprived of much of the information to which the public of a free nation is entitled.'*

Case:	
Goodwin v United Kingdom [1996] 22 ECHR 123	*'Protection of journalistic sources is one of the basic conditions for press freedom ... Without such protection, sources may be deterred from assisting the press in informing the public on matters of public interest. As a result the vital public-watchdog role of the press may be undermined and the ability of the press to provide accurate and reliable information may be adversely affected.'*

However, the release of information to a journalist by a source may amount to a civil wrong such as a breach of confidence. Under such circumstances, a journalist may be required to reveal their source under what is known as a Norwich Pharmacal Order. This states that if a person becomes involved in a wrongful act – such as a journalist receiving confidential information – they come under a duty to assist the person who has been wronged by revealing the identity of the wrongdoer.

Case:	
Norwich Pharmacal Co v Customs and Excise Commissioners [1974] AC 133	Lord Reid: *'If through no fault of his own a person gets mixed up in the tortious acts of others so as to facilitate their wrong-doing he may incur no personal liability but he comes under a duty to assist the person who has been wronged by giving him full information and disclosing the identity of the wrongdoers. I do not think that it matters whether he became so mixed up by voluntary action on his part or because it was his duty to do what he did ... [J]ustice requires that he should co-operate in righting the wrong if he unwittingly facilitated its perpetration.'*

However, s 10 of the Contempt of Court Act 1981 appears to offer some protection to journalists against having to reveal their sources.

Section 10 – Sources of Information
No court may require a person to disclose, nor is any person guilty of contempt of court for refusing to disclose, the source of information contained in a publication for which he is responsible, unless it be established to the satisfaction of the court that disclosure is necessary in the interests of justice or national security or for the prevention of disorder or crime.

That is, it is not a contempt of court for a journalist to refuse to reveal her sources unless a court establishes to its own satisfaction that it is necessary in the interests of justice, national security or for the prevention of disorder or crime.

While s 10 appears to give reasonably wide protection to journalists' sources, the courts have construed the section quite narrowly. Moreover, it seems as though the UK courts and the European Court of Human Rights take different views about the level of protection that should be afforded to journalists' sources. This difference is evident in the following cases.

Cases:	
***X v Morgan Grampian (Publishers) Ltd* [1991] 1 AC 1 *Goodwin v United Kingdom* [1996] 22 EHRR 123**	Note: This is the same case – *X v Morgan Grampian* was the name of the case when heard by the House of Lords whereas *Goodwin v United Kingdom* was the name given to the case when heard by the European Court of Human Rights.
	Facts: Goodwin, a journalist, was passed details of a company's business plan. The company obtained an injunction to prevent the publication of these details. It then sought an order to compel Goodwin to reveal his source.
	Held by the House of Lords:
	It was in the 'interests of justice' as per s 10 of the Contempt of Court Act 1981 for Goodwin to reveal his source. The word 'justice' was not confined to legal proceedings but also meant allowing people to enforce their legal rights against wrongdoers which falls short of bringing an action in a court of law. Their Lordships also held that the importance of protecting a particular journalistic source is weakened by that source's wrongdoing in committing a breach of confidence.

	Held by the European Court of Human Rights:
	The order to reveal the source was a breach of the Article 10 Convention right of freedom of expression. The Court accepted that the order was prescribed by law and sought to achieve a legitimate aim in protecting the company's interests. However, it held that this protection had been sufficiently achieved by the injunction. Thus, the order to reveal the source was not necessary and the company's desire to identify the source did not outweigh the public interest in protecting it.
Interbrew SA v Financial Times and Others [2002] EWCA Civ 274 Financial Times Ltd and Others v The United Kingdom [2010] EMLR 21	Note: this is the same case – *Interbrew SA v Financial Times* was the name of the case when heard by the Court of Appeal whereas *Financial Times Ltd and Others v The United Kingdom* was the name given to the case when heard by the European Court of Human Rights.
	Facts: Interbrew commissioned a confidential report concerning the feasibility of taking over another company: South African Breweries. An unknown source passed the report to a number of newspapers. It is alleged that the report was altered by the source. The newspapers published details of the report, which caused share prices in Interbrew to fall and those in South African Breweries to rise. Interbrew sought an order that the report be returned by the newspapers to enable the source of the leak to be identified.
	Held by the Court of Appeal:
	The newspapers should return the report. The source had committed a wrongful act and so the necessary aspects for a Norwich Pharmacal Order were present. Section 10 of the Contempt of Court Act 1981 could not protect the source. This was because, the Court assumed, the purpose of the leak was spite or profit. In addition, there was evidence that the report had been altered and there was no public interest in protecting those who disseminate false information.

| Held by the European Court of Human Rights: |
| The order that the newspapers should return the report breached their Article 10 rights. An order to reveal a journalistic source would only be legitimate if there were no other, less invasive way to protect Interbrew's interests. While misconduct on behalf of the source was a factor to take into account when considering whether to order disclosure, it was only one factor. Moreover, the ECtHR held that there was insufficient evidence for the UK courts to conclude with the requisite degree of certainty that the source had doctored the report or acted for an improper purpose. |

We can see, then, that in both the *Goodwin* and *Interbrew* cases, the European Court of Human Rights seems more willing to protect journalists' sources than the UK courts.

In both cases, when balancing the public interest in protecting the source (and the consequent protection this gives to freedom of expression) against the interest that the source be revealed, the European Court of Human Rights attaches more weight to the former than does the UK courts.

Workpoint

Produce an essay plan challenging the assertion that there is a difference of approach between UK courts and the European Court of Human Rights with regard to the level of protection that should be given to journalists' sources.

Checkpoint – The protection of journalistic sources

Item on checklist:	Done!
I can explain why the protection of journalistic sources is considered an important ingredient in the guarantee of a free press.	
I can explain why a Norwich Pharmacal Order may force a journalist to disclose their sources.	

Checkpoint – The protection of journalistic sources

Item on checklist:	Done!
I can explain what a court must be satisfied of under s 10 of the Contempt of Court Act 1981 before it may hold a person in contempt of court for refusing to reveal the source of the information on which they have relied.	
I can explain why the UK courts and the European Court of Human Rights appear to have taken different approaches with regard to the protection of journalists' sources.	

Potential exam question

Alex is the editor and owner of the Daily Blab. Alison is running for election as Police Commissioner. It is a significant part of Alison's election campaign that police corruption needs to be eradicated. Alex writes an article supporting Alison and arguing that any police officers found guilty of corruption should be heavily sentenced. In the article, he names PC Muir as deserving of such treatment. The article is published on the third day of Muir's trail for various crimes of police corruption. The Attorney General seeks an order of the court for contempt of court under s 2 of the Contempt of Court Act 1981.

Alex seeks your advice. Explain to him why his article might amount to contempt of court. Also, advise him on any possible defences available to him and of their likelihood of success.

Index